START WITH YOU

START WITH YOU

LEAD FROM THE INSIDE

BELINDA BROSNAN

Copyright © Belinda Brosnan 2018

First published in 2018 by Baker Street Press | Melbourne

ISBN 9780648281207

A catalogue record for this book is available from the National Library of Australia

Edited by Joanna Yardley at The Editing House

Cover design by Helene Webb

This book uses case studies to enforce the meaning behind its relevant chapter. Names have been omitted or changed to protect individual privacy.

Every effort has been made to trace (and seek permission for use of) the original source of material used within this book. Where the attempt has been unsuccessful, the publisher would be pleased to hear from the author/publisher to rectify any omission.

Contents

It's time to wake up

'Your visions will become clear, only
when you can look into your own heart.
Who looks outside, dreams,
who looks inside, awakes.'
—C.G. Jung

In January 2018, I met Ganga, the master trainer for The Hunger Project in Rajasthan, India. Nothing short of a powerhouse, Ganga works with elected women representatives from the Dalit caste leading their local panchayat (the equivalent of our local council). She develops their leadership skills and supports them to access government schemes that are available for their local communities. Her passion for this comes from her own personal circumstances. As a young girl, she had a dream to continue studying; however, her parents had other ideas.

Married at the age of 17, Ganga began to have children and with a two-month-old baby, Ganga managed to convince her family to let her continue studying and get a job. The activist that employed her let her bring her baby to work, which is an extraordinary gesture in an era and country where women are not encouraged to work but to remain home, unseen and unheard.

I asked Ganga when she knew she was meant to be a trainer. "I was told that I was very good, so I made a decision to invest in that strength". To this day, Ganga continually researches ideas online, and experiments to get the best possible outcome for the women she so passionately trains. Women who have been married as young as six and seven years of age, now have a voice because of the extraordinary determination, passion, responsibility, and continual learning mindset and mastery of Ganga's work. Ganga's story is an example of finding a natural talent from the feedback of others and then investing in it continually. She never stopped mastering her art, and she never rested on her laurels or let her ego take over. Her focus is on her passion and purpose to lift some of the most vulnerable and oppressed women, so they can find their own voice and achieve incredible things for their community. The ripple effect is inspiring.

Our wiring as human beings is to seek certainty, comfort, and safety, which is the complete opposite of what is today's and tomorrow's reality: complexity, change, and uncertainty. Ganga had to overcome these incredible challenges to get to where she is today. She is a world class trainer working in some of the most impoverished communities and creating the most courageous leaders I've ever met.

The fire that burned within Ganga burns within all of us. The only difference is that Ganga's flame burned from the age of six. She knew education was the gap that would help her achieve her dreams, and she pursued it relentlessly.

I work with many people in leadership roles whose 'personal light' has been dimmed. You could say some are even 'walking dead': dragging their feet from one meeting or job to the next, unable to pinpoint exactly what it is that has led them to that point. They have a deep sense that they are capable of more; they want to contribute more yet, they are stuck.

Many have had the flame burning for some time but have kept it hidden. Now, they are ready to step up to another level but they can't figure out what is holding them back—they are trying to find their voice and purpose in the world.

This book is a call to wake up.

Gratitudes

Recently, I was privileged to see Dr Bob Bays present to a group of Thought Leaders in Sydney. One of the things that made his talk so powerful was he began with a focus on gratitude, and I love that books start the same way.

Firstly, thank you to my parents Pat and Barb Brosnan who give me so many opportunities and continue to keep me entertained and grounded. You are both real-life versions of leading life by example. To Des, Cath, Paul, and Anita, thank you for your love and all the laughs. Lachlan, Caitlin, Grace, Annie, Joseph, and Thomas (my nieces and nephews), you continue to remind me why I do this work. I want you to grow up in a world filled with positive role models of leadership and teaching, who encourage you to be self-expressed and to be the best versions of yourselves.

I would also like to thank my friends of which there are too many to mention here. Special mentions though to Marie Bata, Geoff Bianci, Karen James, Melanie Noden, Lis Dingjan, Craig Di Lizio, Dominique Williams, Brad Coombs, Tim Redway, Damien Dennis, Riccardo Rizzalli and the crew at DC8 Studio. Ray Fisk and Louise Perram-Fisk for your unconditional love and a home-away-from-home when I needed to be fed married food. Louise, I could never have written a book like this without your inspiration, wisdom and 100 percent unconditional friendship. You are the epitome of living a life that shines light on others. Mandy Lear, thank you wild amigo for cheering me along when I wanted to give up, and for the countless breakfasts spent drawing models and ideas in moleskin notebooks. Kate Cogill, thank you for more than 30 years of friendship and laughter. I still believe your second career is writing. You entertain and support me continually and for that I'm always grateful.

Thanks to all my clients who have done this work with me and proven that amazing things can be achieved. Your expansion as leaders of your own life and the way in which you bravely confront setbacks are why I do this work. Thank you for trusting me to push you out of your comfort zones—I am excited for your futures.

I'd also like to thank my amazing colleagues and mentors who have helped me get to the point where I believed it was possible to write a book and to do the work I do in my own business. Oscar Trimboli, Jane Anderson, Tracey Ezard, Dr Richard Hodge, Corrinne Armour, Paul Worth, Emily Verstege, Digby Scott, Dan Collins, Ritchie Gibson and Dan Gregory, your support has been game changing for me. To Matt Church and Peter Cook, thank you for creating a community that truly depicts what it means for a rising tide to lift all boats.

Thank you to Josie Thomson who was the original inspiration for me to study neuroscience and to Cathy Burke for giving me the opportunity to pursue my passion further with The Hunger Project as a facilitator of the leadership immersion programs in Africa and India.

Last but not least, the extraordinary team around me who helped bring this book to life: Helene Webb, Louise Harrison and Jo Yardley. Thank you.

Introduction

Six years ago, I jumped from the corporate world into my own business. At the time, I was exhausted from running on a treadmill of 'busy', and I couldn't see a way out. My work in property development was exciting and fast paced; however, after 15 years in that industry, I had lost touch with the things that really mattered to me. I knew what I no longer wanted but what I couldn't figure out was *what I wanted to do next.*

One of the biggest revelations I had upon leaving the corporate sector was when I was attending a function where I wasn't there on behalf of any 'big brand' company. I was there as me. And boy it was confronting. I suddenly realised I had seen the organisations I worked for as a huge part of my own identity. I was proud of where I worked but a little too much pride can adversely feed the ego. I was (and still am) a hard worker, which was ingrained in me at a very young age. What crept up on me though was how much I had neglected the things I was passionate about: international travel, creativity and relationships. It was a moment of reset and rebuild for me, and I know from talking with clients since then, that they have had similar moments. I remember my coach at the time asking me, 'What do you want to do?'. My response was anything but graceful, 'I don't give a shit; I'm exhausted'. 'A great place to start,' she replied.

The experience I gained while working in property development during the global financial crisis is invaluable to where I am now. It was a challenging time spent navigating teams to work in an environment where, all of sudden, nothing was certain and the boom times were well and truly gone. That period challenged my own leadership, and it is no surprise that today I am working in the field of leadership development. I have a renewed sense of purpose and a passion for how the brain impacts the way we lead others—more importantly, how we lead ourselves first.

There is a leader inside each of us. I have written this book because I believe that, more than ever, we need great leaders in all aspects of our life: community, work, family, and home. We also need to have braver conversations. Our understanding of how the brain impacts the way we lead is extraordinary, and our knowledge in this field is expanding daily. I want to make this knowledge accessible to everyone with a burning desire to do great things in the world, as those are often the ones most riddled with self-doubt. Not because they don't necessarily believe in themselves, but because they are operating in a new world of work that is complex, uncertain, and ever changing. They want to make a difference. They have a curiosity that drives them to find better ways. When you question everything on the outside, you naturally begin to question yourself but this is also a quality that the leaders of the future need to succeed. This takes courage.

Leadership can be learned if people are committed to the process, have the right mindset, and are given the tools and support to find their voice. Personal and professional leadership are not mutually exclusive. They go hand-in-hand, and this is why I wrote this book. Leadership development programs are falling short of delving deeply into the importance of personal leadership—or leading yourself. The importance of expansive leadership based on evidence from neuroscience has never been more important. Life is too short to be surrounded by uninspired leaders, and to live a life short of extraordinary, whatever that is for you, is doing yourself a disservice. I hope this book helps you uncover the leader within by providing the practical tools and steps to find it.

PART 1

Navigating personal leadership

As a woman who grew up in regional Queensland, it was embedded in my upbringing to make things practical. This book is no different in its style. I've set out *Start with You* with easy to follow (practical) steps to help you find the leader within.

Part 1 of this book outlines how to tune in to who you are and the emergent properties of personal leadership: insight, connection and progress. This is an opportunity to assess where you are right now and where you want to be. It also highlights the importance of social, emotional, and conversational intelligence in personal leadership.

The Step-Up Ladder is a tool for you to identify where you are in your own leadership. Starting at *autopilot*, it will help you to move through *aware* to reach *abundant* in your leadership. By moving through these stages, you will progress from being *locked* to *leveraged* in your capacity as a leader. Ultimately, moving through these stages enables you to first lead yourself, then others.

Mindset overarches personal leadership and is important across all stages. Your mindset is inherently linked to also having an understanding of neuroscience and how the brain influences our thoughts, feelings, and behaviours. Understanding the impact of bias is also an important part of the subtle distinctions of personal leadership.

By setting strong foundations up front, you can begin to unlock possibility. Let's get started.

ONE

Personal leadership starts from within

'All the ugly stereotypes of bad leadership
are expressions of lousy self-leadership.'
—Dan Rockwell, *leadershipfreak.com (empowering
leaders 300 words at a time)*

In leading others through this incredible shifting world, we first need to acknowledge and understand our own humanity so we can show compassion for those with whom we work, and more importantly, for ourselves. We must question our autopilot behaviours and make more informed decisions. Human beings are wired for social connection, and as we exit an era where industrialisation has been the biggest influence on leadership within companies, we need to be prepared to lead differently in the future. Command and control leadership styles will not survive the future of work.

This is why before you even contemplate leading others you need to have the courage and curiosity to lead yourself first. If you have expectations of others to behave in certain ways or do certain things:

are *you* willing to behave in the same way? Leadership for the 21st century is, and will continue to be, anchored in discomfort, so get ready for the ride—cruise control is no longer a viable option.

Tune in: Who are you?

The Dalai Lama once said, "When you talk, you are only repeating what you already know. But if you listen, you may learn something new". Often, we think about this concept in relation to how we connect with others. However, do you apply this to yourself? How often do you stop to listen and tune in to yourself?

We know that curiosity builds connection with others, and this ability to be actively present in the moment and curious about those around us is ultimately the best way for us to connect with them. However, it's also just as applicable to how you lead and connect into yourself. The ability to be in-tune with who you are, to be present in the moment and without judgment, is vital for you to become great at leading yourself and others.

We're often our own worst enemies, and as a result, there are three things that are important in setting ourselves up for success and tuning in to who we really are. When we don't take the time to go through these steps, risks appear and divert us away from the best opportunity for personal leadership.

1. Assess

The first important aspect of personal leadership is the ability to **assess**. This means to raise your head above the water regularly to see what is on the horizon. It's about looking beyond the day-to-day towards possibility. Too often, we limit ourselves by not taking time for reflection. When you're able to assess where you are, you can see how you appear as you step up in your own personal leadership. This is why the best leaders have coaches. The power of reflection in a busy world is often what helps us elevate to the next level.

When we don't take time to assess where we are at, we are at risk of:

- becoming disengaged
- making assumptions and losing opportunities in the process
- lacking awareness of what is really going on
- missing the big picture.

TUNE IN: ASSESS WHERE YOU ARE AT RIGHT NOW

Thinking about your life today, what are some of the things you want to achieve?

What insights do you have into the things that are holding you back from achieving these goals? (*perhaps you don't even know what these goals are?)

Where is your focus right now?

How is this impacting the way you connect with others?

What are your strengths as a leader?

How might your strengths also, at times, present themselves as a weakness?

What's your impact on others?

What have you assumed people know about you?

What's truly possible for you if you were to explore your own leadership?

Are you listening to your own voice? Are you scared to pursue an opportunity that is calling you?

You can't be what you can't see. Who can help you expand your thinking?

2. Align

The second step is to **align** yourself with what matters most to you. Your core values and your energy are key to unlocking what your real goals may be and will give you insight into the places where you may be misaligned. If the concept of family is a high value, yet you spend excessive hours at your desk because the company norm is 'face time' (the notion that you could only be hard working if you are seen at your desk until late at night every day), you are not aligned, and you are projecting poor role-modelling. Being able to identify when you aren't aligned is a critical skill for all leaders. When you're aligned, you're more likely to be congruent. Alignment also means learning to set boundaries.

When we aren't in alignment the following occurs:

- ☀ We feel an internal conflict, uncertainty, and unease.
- ☀ We may also be incoherent, not really making sense, not clear on what it is that we're doing. Our autopilot behaviours take over and move us into short-term tactical approaches in the way we lead.
- ☀ Our focus may be in the wrong place.

Understanding our values and why they are important is key when checking our alignment. When I left my corporate role in 2011, I had suddenly taken the time to reflect on what really mattered to me and what my preferences and priorities were? The ability to stop, pause, and reflect on this was central to my decision to go out on my own. I knew that if values such as freedom, creativity, making a difference, connection, generosity, and courage were important for me, then I must show up in an organisation where those values were aligned—or alternatively in my own business.

Not being in alignment can trigger rumination: thoughts that track over and over in our head, and potentially put us into a 'threat' response and 'protection' mindset. When we are in this state and we're not aligned; we are ultimately acting from the emotional brain, which means we move into distrust of ourselves and others. We try to mitigate threats. We aren't focused on what is truly possible for us moving forward. It is this lack of alignment that can keep us stuck where we are.

TUNE IN: ALIGN TO YOUR PREFERENCES AND PRIORITIES

If you were living a life that was aligned with your values and purpose, what would you be doing differently?

To what level do others influence your behaviour and decision making?

How often do you say 'yes' to requests and then feel annoyed later that you didn't say 'no'?

Do you have a nagging sense of something not feeling quite right?

What energises you?

3. Action

The third component of tuning in to who you are is to take **action**. Action is the antidote to confidence. Preparation is what gives us conviction. Coaching as a profession is primarily focused on helping people reach their goals. But what if you don't really know what your goals are? You just know something isn't quite right? If you can move one tiny step forward to explore deeply within, even if you aren't 100 percent clear on your goal, then you are on your way to getting the clarity you need.

Nelson Mandela is famous for saying, "Action without vision is only passing time. Vision without action is merely daydreaming. But when our vision and action are aligned, we can change the world". We are *how* we show up, not how we *intend* to show up.

When we don't take action we can:

- 'freeze'
- procrastinate
- begin to show resistance, and sometimes we're not sure why
- allow self-doubt and limiting beliefs to take over.

When self-doubt takes over, we lose our ability to connect and ultimately lead.

When you can assess, align, and take action—and ensure that you have all three working together—you gain the insight you need to build true connection with others and to make progress.

((U)) TUNE IN: TAKE ACTION, EVEN IF YOUR
GOALS AREN'T 100 PERCENT CLEAR

Pablo Picasso once said that 'action is the foundational key to all success'. What habit or mindset do you need to let go of to take your first step forward to being a better leader of yourself?

What is one action you can take to move forward?

Insight, connection, and progress

There are three emergent properties of personal leadership that are the focus underneath every chapter of this book. These emergent properties ensure your personal leadership propels into the future.

In our hyper-connected world of 'busy', we're primed for losing insight into ourselves, others, and opportunities. Great leaders make the time for exploration so they can remain focused on the things that matter most. Insight is intentional and conscious. It is deliberate, and this mindfulness is what takes us out of autopilot behaviours that might feel efficient in the moment but ultimately lead us to a mindless operating model that inhibits our ability to influence others and ourselves.

INSIGHT is overlooked in a world where busy is the boss and sometimes a badge of honour. Checking in and reflecting are critical elements to personal leadership and well-being that place us on the pathway to seeing what's possible for us. *Without a moment to pause, we chase the wrong cause.*

INSIGHT: BEFORE AND AFTER

WITHOUT INSIGHT	WITH INSIGHT
Way I've always done things	Trying new things and innovating
Weakness fixing	Leveraging and building your strengths
Raw emotion without care of others	Regulated emotion with care
Purpose and values difficult to articulate	Clear on core values and purpose
Wrong focus and attention: attachment to concerns/ worrying about things can't control	Focus and attention on things within my influence and control
Incongruent: creating distrust	Congruence of mind and body: priming trust
Ego driven	Humility and service
Make assumptions	Mindful and curious
Disengaged	Engaged

CONNECTION is the second emergent property of personal leadership. Too often, people fall into the trap of 'existing' not 'living'. Taking the time to stop and be present with others in the moment, and being curious about them as people is the essence of true connection with others. *Power with others, not over others.*

CONNECTION: BEFORE AND AFTER

WITHOUT CONNECTION	WITH CONNECTION
Exclusion: isolate others outside your 'in-group'	Inclusion: make an effort to invite people in
Ad hoc with stakeholders	Strategic in your approach to key stakeholders
Doing everything alone: feeling isolated	Being resourceful: inviting others in to help, feeling energised
'Me' focused	'We' focused
Shut down and judgmental	Open and curious
Homogenous networks: limited to people like me	Diverse networks: reaching outside your comfort zone to include people who stretch you and pull you toward your goals

With the introduction of technology in particular, we've lost the art of connecting with others in meaningful ways. While there are elements of technology that have brought us closer globally, they also bring challenges by disconnecting us from others face-to-face.

Technology can be a huge distraction rendering our ability to connect genuinely with others almost impossible. Things go wrong when we don't pay attention to the purpose of our connection, or when we don't listen, or when we're too fearful of speaking transparently. As humans, our need to feel certain, or to control, compounds our love of *being right*. Because of this, connection requires great self-awareness and regulation. While we're fundamentally human, we can improve the way we connect with others by paying attention to our common purpose, by having the courage to speak our truth, by display curiosity, and by holding genuine conversations. Humans are wired for social connection, so it's essential that you first connect with yourself.

PROGRESS over perfection. Too often we hold ourselves back based on self-doubt and limiting beliefs. When we think we have to be perfect, the pressure is immense and comparison drives our actions. When you focus on what you need to do *to move one step forward*, the pressure eases and all of sudden you have movement.

PROGRESS: BEFORE AND AFTER

WITHOUT PROGRESS	WITH PROGRESS
Procrastinating and feeling stuck	Moving forward
Self-doubt and limiting self-beliefs	Willingness to take risks even if there is the possibility of failure or rejection
Perfection: needing to be perfect or do something perfectly	Purposeful progress equals 'good enough'
Withdrawn: don't speak up	Self-expressed: able to articulate your thoughts, feelings and beliefs
Fear driven	Possibility driven
Invisible intentions	Visible intent and considered impact

George Bernard Shaw once said, "Progress is impossible without change, and those who cannot change their minds cannot change anything". Progress that is tangible and meaningful will continue to fuel your personal motivation. Intention is invisible, and therefore, if we are going to be great leaders, we need to translate our intention into progress or action. As Dan Pink talked about in Drive (2011), research shows that the simple act of searching for one's own answers, which is an element of insight problem-solving, has the ability to engage us. These insights are memorable due to their emotional quality. They help us retain what we've learned, and they activate the brain reward system. We are all fundamentally human, and improving our personal leadership is leveraged when we become conscious of the above. When you delve below the surface, to tune truly into who you are, an important part of personal leadership is starting to unlock possibility through this emotional maturity.

Personal leadership intelligence

Personal leadership is as much an art as it is a science because it requires a level of insight to evaluate your own vulnerability and humanity, as well as having the leadership intelligence to distinguish the subtleties of personal leadership distinctions. This is where social, emotional, and conversational intelligence come into play.

Social intelligence

Social intelligence is about our interpersonal intelligence: how well we interact with others and our ability to invoke cooperation. According to Tom Rath, author of Strengths Based Leadership (2009), people follow those who provide hope, stability, trust, and compassion. Social intelligence taps into this implicitly. It is the ability to realise that your role as a leader is to inspire the people you lead and with whom you work.

It also requires the ability for wider organisational awareness. In leading yourself, there are times when your own 'mission' must be timed strategically. I learned this from sitting on the floor of a room with elected panchayat women leaders from the lowest Dalit caste in remote villages in India. These women desperately want to see the end of practices such as self-selective abortion (aborting girls as they are considered 'not of value') and child marriage. However, if they started their election campaigns focused on this, the chances of their election and support through their 5-year tenure may be limited. First, they focus on what the community needs to build trust. They manage this through achievements like providing running water and working roads to their villages. After they have earned a reputation and respect, they can proceed with more challenging societal issues such as self-selective abortion and child marriage.

This is no different in our organisations and businesses. It's not always possible to have our needs met first. Those who lead themselves well, know how to look strategically at the context of a situation to determine the missions and battles to pursue, to let go, or to set aside for now. **Social intelligence is about choosing your battles wisely.**

When leaders get fixated on their own 'patch' rather than the wider organisation, they often lose influence among their peers and those they need to influence up. Social intelligence is tied intrinsically to relationships. If leaders ignore relationships and their importance in human connection, they miss the true opportunity to grow their leadership and career. We are wired as human beings to connect, and it is needed in our organisations today more than ever as evidenced by Gallup's *State of the Global Workplace* study in 2013. The report showed that in Australia, three in four Australian employees are not 'engaged' at work. Worse still, they discovered that the 16 percent who are 'actively disengaged' cost the nation approximately $54.8 billion annually. We need leaders in Australia to turn these statistics around.

Emotional intelligence

At the heart of personal leadership is self-awareness and management, or emotional intelligence. Dr Karl Albrecht defines emotional intelligence as self-insight and the ability to regulate or manage one's reactions to experience. Daniel Goleman, author of *Emotional Intelligence*, describes emotional and social intelligence as having four key competencies including self-awareness, self-management, social awareness and relationship management. People with high emotional intelligence are highly tuned-in to their internal world. This is where, as a leader, compassion is developed for yourself and others.

The obvious metaphor for this is the safety demonstration on an aircraft of *fitting your own oxygen mask before you assist others*. What are you doing to maintain your mojo? What are your 'triggers' for ensuring you keep this in check? For example, as a self-confessed extrovert, I know I'm in the grip of stress when I start to isolate myself and avoid others. While I also need time alone to refuel my energy tank, when I let that go on for too long, that's my 'trigger' to pull myself back into equilibrium. I do this by reaching out to someone in my tribe, or I increase my exercise as that is what boosts my fuel tank.

Leaders often forget self-compassion and self-care. Developing the emotional intelligence to regulate ourselves, allows us to also deliver the same compassion to others.

Conversational intelligence

The third intelligence essential for personal leadership development is conversational intelligence. CIQ Conversational Intelligence was developed by Judith E Glaser. She defines conversational intelligence as "the hardwired and learnable ability to connect, navigate and grow with others – a necessity in building healthier and more resilient organisations in the face of change. It begins with elevating the level of trust that you create with people and ends with the quality of interactions and conversations that result".

To have quality conversations, leaders need the power to trust themselves to explore and ask questions to which they don't know the answer. When we ask questions that can instill uncertainty within ourselves, it can provoke a feeling of threat or a sense of discomfort in case we get an answer to which we do not know how to respond. If the conversation becomes 'positional', where the focus is on trying to sell our idea to someone else, the brain can initially be rewarded as it makes us feel good to be right. When we understand the impact of being addicted to being right, we can suspend our attachment to things and open up our curiosity to different ways of thinking or different ideas.

Are you addicted to being right? Beginning to recognise this matters. It's one of your first steps to setting the foundations for conversations anchored in transparency, courage, and kindness. It is also the hallmark of expansive personal leadership.

Two

Stages of personal leadership development

In my experience, leaders seeking to develop their leadership skills are often surprised at how much of their own personal development is essential to build their professional development. Professional development without personal leadership development is bound to be fruitless. Before you can lead others, you must be able to lead yourself first. If who you are at work and at home are two different people, then you are setting yourself up for pain, stress, and exhaustion.

People who can lead themselves know that leading yourself well means bringing your best self to all situations. They are like magnets who attract others to them. You might not share your personal life with those at work; however, that is not the same as 'being a different person' at work and home. When I hear people express this, I know that there is a world of pain lying beneath the surface and often their performance at work is below average.

Over the past six years of running my own business, I have learned that we are capable of much more than we realise. What challenges us is our perception of what our true capacity is. This book will give you the tools to move from autopilot to abundance, by becoming conscious of your leadership of yourself and of others, and by unlocking your true capabilities and ultimately, capacity.

The path to personal leadership and growth moves across three stages on the Step-Up Ladder.

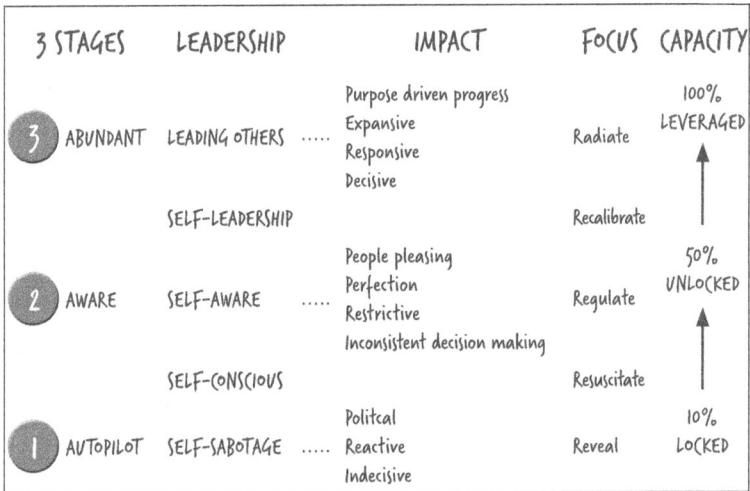

THE STEP-UP LADDER

3 STAGES	LEADERSHIP	IMPACT	FOCUS	CAPACITY
3 ABUNDANT	LEADING OTHERS	Purpose driven progress Expansive Responsive Decisive	Radiate	100% LEVERAGED ↑
	SELF-LEADERSHIP		Recalibrate	
2 AWARE	SELF-AWARE	People pleasing Perfection Restrictive Inconsistent decision making	Regulate	50% UNLOCKED ↑
	SELF-CONSCIOUS		Resuscitate	
1 AUTOPILOT	SELF-SABOTAGE	Politcal Reactive Indecisive	Reveal	10% LOCKED

Figure 1: Personal leadership starts from within

Stage one: Autopilot

Leaders operating on autopilot are often stuck on a treadmill of busy. They appear as little hermits relentlessly chasing ... well, what exactly are they chasing? They're not sure themselves sometimes as they are often reactionary to what is going on around them. At their worst, leaders on autopilot self-sabotage themselves. They may fall into the trap of political behaviour, and they are often highly-emotive and reactionary to people and situations that they don't approve of or fully understand.

They have little ability to read the play and believe the stories and movies playing out in their heads to be the truth.

When leaders are in the autopilot stage of leadership development, they can exhibit the following behaviours:

- Engaging in 'political' behaviour such as white-anting or blindsiding others.
- Allowing insecurities to show up as emotional explosion in the workplace.
- Being reactive and often running at a fast pace with little thought for those around them.
- Being continually distracted by 'screen time' or scrolling the internet. Technology trumps their connection with others.
- Allowing self-doubt to consume them. They start to question their career decisions and may feel lost or helpless.
- Allowing their evaluation of experiences to be subjective: when things don't go well, they do 'what feels right' rather than 'what is most needed'. (Schwartz, et al., 2016)
- Engaging in poor decision making, or not making decisions based on binary thinking: an all-or-nothing approach.
- Paying little attention to their 'intentions' and the ultimate impact on others.
- Feeling that life is moving out of control.

The autopilot stage of leadership is the least conscious. Our brain loves to reside there. It uses up less energy, it's comfortable and efficient. The brain never stops. This is significant for how we operate as humans because our brain is approximately two percent of our body weight and uses around 20–25 percent of our body's energy. Our emotional brain (more specifically the amygdala and limbic system), in very simple terms, is wired to keep us safe and has evolved from the caveman days when we needed to detect whether you were friend or foe. It also relies on existing 'maps' in the brain to predict the future. Our memory is stored in the limbic system. This is why, at times, when you are driving a car you may reflect on the past 20 minutes of driving and realise that you have no memory of the journey. This is because your brain is on autopilot. It is using old existing maps in the brain to get stuff done. In this instance, to drive your car from A to B.

When leaders are on autopilot, they often miss what is really going on around them. They can't detect subtle emotion and body language queues that allow them to make better decisions. Then there is 'inattentional blindness'. When we are asked to perform a challenging task, without realising it, our attention narrows and blocks out other things.

In 2013, researchers Trafton Drew and Jeremy Wolfe from Harvard University engaged a team of radiologists to review images of lung scans that happened to have an image of a gorilla placed in the top right of the image.[1]

Each radiologist was tested to determine what percentage would notice the gorilla in the corner. 83 percent of radiologists did not see the gorilla. Why is that? Radiologists are trained to look for cancer. Even when they looked at the image, the researchers used retina technology to determine whether their eye had looked at the gorilla and every single one of them had, yet 83 percent didn't register that it was there.

In the words of Helen Turnbull, a leading diversity expert, "the unchallenged brain is not to be trusted". So despite the incredible ability of our human brain, this also highlights our fragility as human beings if

1 (You can view the image at https://www.ncbi.nlm.nih.gov/pmc/articles/ PMC3964612/).

we don't become more mindful and present. Jeffrey Schwartz and Josie Thomson refer to it as being able to decipher between deceptive brain messages and using 'our wise advocate'. This is why being conscious in your leadership is so crucial.

As human beings in the state of autopilot, there are four key characteristics of being human that get in the way of leaders reaching their true potential.

1. Our need to belong

Being human means we have a need for social connection and to belong. Our need for social connection and belonging is often what gets in the way of us speaking our truth, having a tough conversation or giving an independent opinion in a meeting. In fact, we know from neuroscientists and pschologists that our need to belong is considered more powerful than fear in driving our behaviour. It's the thing that stops us speaking up, being vulnerable or willing to admit our mistakes, and not willing to move against the crowd.

2. Comfort zone

Our brain loves comfort zones and the efficiency that comes with doing things on autopilot. Autopilot modes of operation result in default behaviours that occur when the limbic system and the fast or reflexive system (also known as our X system) take over. These hardwired responses are characterised by their sensory and automatic nature and can impede personal leadership as the brain is not accessing the prefrontal cortex associated with critical thinking and wise decision making. Comfort zones can often lead to poor decision making and lazy leadership. We need to interrupt those patterns.

3. Fear

As human beings, we're wired to detect threat over reward. Fear is the primary operating principle of the brain that drives autopilot behaviours. As David Rock from the NeuroLeadership Institute once said, "what you expect is what you experience". Your emotional brain is a strong force behind why you avoid stepping up in your leadership. Instead of fighting it, work with it; be curious about what is making you feel that way.

The limbic system is part of the fast, reflexive system that triggers fear based emotional responses such as fight, flight, freeze, and defense. The overarching drive to minimise threat rather than maximising reward has significant consequences to how we work together. These consequences can be catastrophic when leaders and people at work don't have the training, knowledge or skills required to build resilience against inappropriate activated stressors.

Our disposition to 'threat over reward' and learned fear also predisposes us to negative bias. This, along with the suppression of emotion, can have negative impacts on leadership and decision-making including our ability to have insight, think logically, make good decisions, and be creative and more innovative. When in the grip of a threat response, we tend to err on the side of pessimism and generalise threat as our first response to a situation. This is driven by the limbic system rather than our prefrontal cortex that is critical for our executive function. When we lead using our prefrontal cortex, we can undertake functions such as planning, reasoning, decision-making, thinking and awareness of others and the future. However, if our emotional brain or 'limbic system' overtakes this executive function when under perceived threat, then our ability to make wise leadership decisions can be compromised.

4. Control

The fourth influencer of auto-pilot behaviours is our desire for certainty and to maintain control of our lives. Letting go, as a leader, doesn't have to mean losing control. Part of regulating this need for certainty, is learning ways to manage ourselves when we feel the need to take control by exerting power over others. Wise leaders know that it is possible to ask great questions we don't know the answers to, without letting our threat responses take hold.

When leaders have power within, they can loosen the grip on control and begin to lead 'with' others which we explore later in this book. This conviction gives them the ability to be okay with challenging their own views and judgments, to set their intentions, to act accordingly, and to let go of the things that get in the way or don't matter. This means that they don't get locked into the past being a predictor of the future. Instead, the past gives them context to look forward and make wise decisions in an environment that is most likely changing and evolving rapidly.

Stage two: Aware

The second stage of personal leadership development is awareness. This stage is challenging for leaders, as they enter a period of 'conscious incompetence' moving towards 'conscious competence'. As leaders move into this stage, they become more aware of their emotional reactions, as well as the influence of 'movie-making' that occurs in the brain, resulting from assumptions and interpretations, and 'meaning making' that we create when trying to predict outcomes. The brain loves certainty and leaders who are aware of this can begin to decipher the difference between their mind and their brain, which takes much effort and can feel overwhelming at times.

Leaders in this stage become aware of the importance of a growth mindset over a fixed mindset to help them through the discomfort of change. Our mindset, according to Carol Dweck is defined as "how your mental attitude and beliefs shape how you respond and interpret situations". In *Mindset: The Psychology of Success* (2006), Carol reveals that those with a *fixed* mindset believe that intelligence is a fixed trait, and as a result of adopting that mindset, they are likely to avoid challenges. They will disregard obstacles as 'too hard' and will see feedback and the success of others as a threat. Ultimately, they will play small.

When we adopt a *growth* mindset, we see effort and learning as the path to growth and mastery. We believe that intelligence can be learned and as a result we are more likely to take on harder tasks, rise to challenges, and see feedback and the success of others as an opportunity to learn and grow.

Mindset is critical to moving through all three phases, especially through the awareness phase into abundance as this is where we try different things. Some will work and some won't but our mindset plays a huge role in leveraging our leadership capacity.

Stage three: Abundant

As we move through autopilot and become aware, we shift up a gear to stage three—being abundant. This final stage is where we have better mastery of self leadership, which is essential for leading others.

The word abundant might feel like a strange expression in relation to leadership. Upon returning home from my first trip to Uganda in 2013 with The Hunger Project, I thought about how people in the villages had transformed their lives by creating their own businesses. It was an incredible lesson in leadership. At the time, I was just starting to work for myself. I was in a true scarcity mindset. *What if I don't earn enough money? What if I fail? What if no one values my work?*

We have an abundance of opportunity and resources available, yet our wiring as human beings is to focus on what we don't have and what we don't want. My way of thinking was disempowering myself. Our culture is also highly materialistic and profit-focused, further reinforcing the 'scarcity' paradigm. The advertising and marketing messages we see every day feed into this mindset reinforcing what we 'don't have'. We don't have enough money, time, holidays—you get the picture.

Leaders moving into the abundant stage focus on *what can I do with what I have?* It's about being expansive and resourceful as leaders. This is the ultimate in mastering personal leadership. It's about moving away from the 'not enough' paradigm that plagues most leaders working through complexity, change and uncertainty.

When our leadership is conscious and purpose driven, we're focused on the right things. We are responsive rather than reactive, and we're decisive because we're clear about what matters deep within us and to our organisations or business. The differentiating point though is that in stage three we have an ability to work with our own humanness by rewiring our brain to focus on what is possible. What can we do with what we have? And beyond that, to become expansive in our impact. Not just for ourselves but also for others. It is not about perfection. It's about the ability to be mindful leaders, being able to recalibrate and refocus on what matters most.

'Authenticity' is potentially an overused and often misunderstood word. However, in my work it is the one word my clients repeatedly hear from their bosses: "We can't believe the change in Jane, yet she's retained who she is and has remained authentic". Doing this work on ourselves can be confronting as moving to stage three requires letting go of our old self and ways of operating. Authenticity as defined by Bill George, author of *Discover your True North* (2015) and a senior fellow at Harvard Business School focuses on character rather than style:

> *People of the highest integrity, committed to building enduring organisations, who have a deep sense of purpose and are true to their core values who have the courage to build their companies to meet the needs of all their stakeholders, and who recognise the importance of their service to society.*

He continues to define authentic leaders as demonstrating the following five qualities:

1. Understanding their purpose
2. Practicing solid values
3. Leading with heart
4. Establishing connected relationships
5. Demonstrating self-discipline.

In his leadership blog, Michael Hyatt, further defines authentic leaders as having five hallmarks including insight, demonstrating initiative, exerting influence, having impact and exercising integrity. Authenticity is not defined as 'being true to yourself' as that implies doing whatever you like at the detriment of everyone else. Personal leadership is about a human-centred approach to leadership development. It is about doing the hard inner-work to develop yourself so you can confront change, uncertainty, and complexity on a solid foundation and with a strong inner-compass. This means adopting things that you feel work, and evolving and expanding your impact based on a willingness to stretch yourself.

I believe authenticity, as defined above, misses two important things a) the importance of being expansive and b) transparency. Transparency is key to building trust as a core foundation to your leadership. Being expansive as a leader is about having the ability to transcend across four paradigms associated with leading through a changing work environment:

- Communities: building connection among people
- Realities: leaning in to issues as they arise, moving to resolution
- Opportunities: the ability to promote and connect strategy and execution in the moment
- Possibilities: navigating the way toward to a better future.

When we have an abundant mindset, we can energetically begin to transform our own leadership. When we are expansive, we take action based on vision for ourselves and others that transcends the status quo, and we ignite possibility when others think something is impossible.

When the light within us is brighter than our need for the light to be on us, we become expansive in our leadership. Just like a flame or light, being abundant is when our light within helps guide others out of the dark. This is the essence of this book.

THREE

Mindset

> 'The view you adapt for
> yourself, profoundly affects the
> way you lead your life.'
> —Dr Carol S. Dweck, *Mindset.*

Your mindset is when your mental attitude and beliefs shape how you respond and interpret situations. Mindset is the birthplace of influence and personal leadership. However, it is frequently overlooked when people are developing their leadership skills. There is a tendency to focus on building communication and presentation skills so you can be confident, or teaching people the skills of feedback. Of course, all these lessons are valuable; however, if you haven't explored mindset first, then you are missing an important part of a person's leadership development. You cannot develop your personal leadership skills if you don't have a conscious awareness of your mindset. Just like your wardrobe, your mindset needs a regular spring clean to stay fresh and on track to achieving your goals.

Mindset impacts your physiology and there are three key mindsets essential for personal leadership that expand on the work of Carol Dweck's 'growth' mindset. Without a mindset that is *abundant, inclusive and possibility* focused, being an abundant leader through change, uncertainty and complexity will become near impossible. As my friend Louise Perram-Fisk says, "you might have a poker face but you will never have a poker body".

If you must connect with and influence a key stakeholder and your mindset about that person is less than favourable, then your body language will show that. They will make that judgment in 0.7 seconds. While they might not be able to identify what you are thinking, they will know if something isn't 'quite right' by how you show up. They can judge you as 'foe' very quickly and this shifts their brain closer to distrust. Then the stakeholder becomes less open to influence.

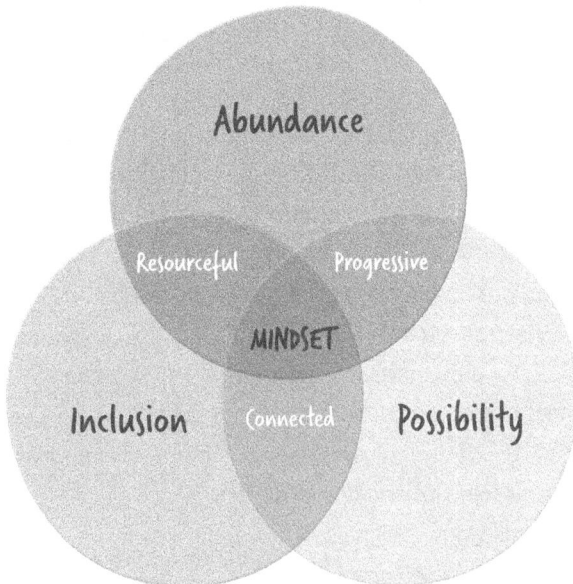

Figure 2: Mindset model for personal leadership

Abundance

A leader with an **abundance** mindset believes in being and having enough or doing the best we can with what we have. This is not about blind optimism, it is based on making the choice to have a mental attitude that will serve you best for the life you want to create for yourself. An abundance mindset is the essence of being resourceful and making progress.

SCARCITY MINDSET	ABUNDANCE MINDSET
I'm not enough.	I'm making the most of what I have.
I don't have enough … (time, money etc.)	What can I do with what I have? I don't have to do it all on my own.
I'm not experienced enough.	I'm learning every day and making progress.
I don't have all the qualifications.	I'll give it my best shot as I believe I can make a difference.
I don't have the time to make it perfect, and I don't want to fail.	I'm making progress and that's more important than perfection.

A scarcity mindset embedded in the 'not enough' internal dialogue keeps you paralysed in indecision and inaction. This, in its own right, is a decision and one that never serves us well. When we consciously shift to an abundance mindset, we naturally begin to focus on what's **possible**.

Possibility

One of the greatest mindset challenges I see in people wanting to develop their leadership, is a mindset of entitlement. Entitlement can be one of the most subtle mindsets to identify. It is the belief that we have a right *to* something or we are right *about* something. This mindset creates barriers, as often we expect people to 'just know this is important' without being explicit in what it is we are seeking. What is obvious to you is not necessarily obvious to another person. Entitlement can be incredibly subtle and foster bitterness, anger, and frustration. Instead fostering a mindset that focuses on what's possible will more often than not, motivate us into positive action.

ENTITLEMENT MINDSET	POSSIBILITY MINDSET
I've worked here X years, so I should get the opportunity.	What can I do to ensure they know I want that opportunity? How can I add value?
They should tell me what my next career goal or move should be.	I'm not clear on my next move, but I know that I have XYZ strengths to contribute and make a difference. This is where I shine.
I work hard; I deserve to be recognised.	Being recognised for my efforts motivates me. I let my manager know this is important to me so we have an understanding of how we can best work together.
I shouldn't have to sell myself; they should know how hard I work.	I've got some clear goals on what I want to achieve. Who are the people that need to know this so I can raise awareness of my aspirations and have a plan of attack to achieve them?

Inclusion

Having an **inclusion** mindset is key to developing your personal leadership. Throughout life, we need to connect with a diverse range of people and situations; however, as humans we are biased to liking people like us. If we don't manage this, it can lead to the creation of 'us and them' interactions as our judgments of others are based on whether they are in our in-group or our out-group. It is crucial to understand this distinction. We judge our in-group by their *intentions* and we judge our out-group by their *impact*. By suspending judgment and listening with genuine curiosity, we can learn a great deal about ourselves and others. It feels risky and uncomfortable, yet it's the birthplace of leadership, influence and connection.

EXCLUSION MINDSET	INCLUSION MINDSET
Their department is obsessed with blocking every initiative we put forward.	Both our departments are passionate about what we do. What is our higher purpose, so we can find a common ground?
They leave me out all the time.	I know they aren't necessarily intending to leave me out, so I'll have the conversation with them as it's important to me that I belong and am included.
I never get the opportunities that they do.	I would like the opportunity to … and I will make it known that it is important to me.

Mindset is a fundamental element of every stage of personal leadership development. **Choose the mindset that will serve you best for the future you want to create.**

Use the table on the next page to 'discover your state'.

DISCOVER YOUR STATE

At first, you may not be aware of your mindset and some of the beliefs that play out in your mind. Over the next few weeks (and to be honest, for life) aim to tune into your thoughts. Diarise in a notebook or in your phone (eg the Evernote app) any thoughts you have that are potentially getting in the way of your success. Do you notice any patterns? Write them here.

_____

_____

_____

_____

If you knew that a thought is just a thought and not a fact, how might that change the way you interpret and respond to situations?

_____

_____

_____

_____

Is there a mindset from above that you want to develop more? (eg Abundance, Possibility or Inclusion.)

_____

_____

_____

_____

How has mindset potentially held you back to date?

_____

_____

_____

_____

Remember the best leaders of themselves and others are *always learning*. They focus on *progress, not perfection*. Start practicing a more abundance, possibility and inclusion mindset. Write your actions below.

_____

_____

_____

_____

Navigating bias

Have you ever had one of those weeks where you feel like every single person you dealt with was difficult? Or that they just 'didn't get it'? The opening line of an end-of-day phone conversation with one of my friends occasionally goes something like this:

> Friend: Did you have to work with the humans today?

> Me: (sigh) ... Yep. I worked with the humans.

While it is intentional, typical, Aussie 'tongue in cheek' humour (directly aimed at the fact that I really enjoy working with all sorts of people), it sums up how many leaders feel about the daily struggle of influencing up, across and down in their organisations. Working with people who *aren't* like us takes effort. Effort can move us into a **fixed** mindset—*this is just how things are*—rather than a **growth** mindset where we would view the situation as an opportunity to learn and grow.

KEY DEFINITIONS:

DEFINING BIAS: Your inclinations or prejudices for or against a person or group, especially in a way that is considered unfair.

COGNITIVE BIAS: Automatic influences on human judgment and decision making that reliably produce reasoning errors.

AFFINITY or INGROUP BIAS: Perceiving people who are similar to you more positively than people who are different from you.

In reality, research shows better business results when there is a mix of people in leadership teams. But what people don't often articulate is that working with a group of different people takes effort. With globalisation, rapid advances in technology and an ageing population, it is certain that we will see more than five generations in the workplace. It is inevitable that you will be working with people who are different from you. Sounds easy when you rattle it off in a sentence; however, as humans we are tribal creatures and **we like people like us.**

Your personal leadership requires you to acknowledge and understand the biases and blind spots that get in the way of you showing up to be your best every day when you are navigating people of all creeds and colours. Do you have biases of some kind? Maybe you think you have no biases?

In essence, we are all biased—if you have a brain, you are biased. It can be conscious and deliberate, and it can also be non-conscious. Your beliefs about various social and identity groups stem from your tendency to put people into categories in an effort to manage all the information coming at you. Often though, you don't consciously realise you are doing it.

There is a popular view that only the *bad guys* are biased and the *good guys* wouldn't do that. But the reality is that all of us have bias no matter who we are. As humans, our need to belong is even more powerful than fear. We are wired for social connection, and the 'heart brain' is where we identify whether someone is friend or foe. Can I trust you or can I not trust you? Are you like me or not? Judith E Glaser in *Conversational Intelligence*, says that we make a judgment in less than 0.7 seconds. This reflexive and fast response is part of our ancient wiring. While we can't control the initial biochemical reaction, or our initial thoughts and feelings, **we do have a choice about what to do with those thoughts and feelings.**

It is for this reason that mindset and knowledge of our innate human biases is the pathway to more conscious leadership practices. When combined with mitigation strategies and a strong focus on developing leaders who are equipped to lead an inclusive culture, leadership is fairer and more equitable.

How we judge people and ourselves

'Our like-mindedness was a
comfort, a shortcut to intimacy.'
—Bill Bishop, *The Big Sort*

Perhaps the most pervasive impact of affinity bias is that we judge our in-groups on their **intentions,** and we judge our out-groups on their **impact**. Think about that for a moment. When have you judged a friend or member of your team who stuffed up more leniently because they were part of your in-group? Alternatively, if a person in your out-group made the same mistake, it would bring outrage and righteousness.

What about your own stuff-ups and errors? How do you judge yourself? For some, the judgment of ourselves is the harshest where others may use phrases like, *I was only joking* or *I didn't mean to do that* or *I didn't intend to harm anyone*. These statements prevent them from taking responsibility.

Think about where you witness this in your organisation. Perhaps it is across function areas creating silos? I witnessed this when working within a banking organisation years ago. Every quarter we held a 'staff update' pre-GFC, where the drinks flowed and no expense was spared to celebrate the company's success. As with any industry, there are always a few who enjoy one too many drinks at a work function. At this particular function, I watched a guy dance in what I can only describe as Lleyton Hewitt meets Mick Jagger: tie wrapped around his forehead, shirt unbuttoned. It was a sight to behold, watching this guy strut up and down the dance floor in front of the entire organisation. I recall one of my real estate colleagues rolling his eyes at me and saying 'Mortgages ... no class!'

This story is not foreign to anyone. We judge and categorise people based on the stereotypes of function, gender, sexuality, education ... the list goes on. The point here is not whether one section of the bank was better than another but rather to highlight that it is automatic to categorise. Our brain compartmentalises people and predicts continually to create certainty. We often don't question it. However, when this judgement impacts business decisions and results, it is pervasive and potentially damaging not only to the organisation but to your own personal leadership and reputation.

Social media is further exacerbating the divide of 'us and them'. You only need to see the torrent of trolls and 'right and wrong' debates under the comments of posts on Facebook and Twitter to sense that we have lost our ability to converse with one another about our differences without it breaking into all-out online warfare. I know from my own brother in the police force, that Facebook is now the cause of many a domestic dispute callout.

Personal leadership requires diversity of thinking that comes from leading people across all spectrums of society. Imagine if it were possible to ride this wave more smoothly? If you could work with multiple generations with more ease and know that your decision making was delivered with more conviction and certainty because you had better awareness of some of your own biases and blind spots.

Bias can impact businesses, and it can make or break the quality of our decisions, our client relationships, and how we lead others, particularly if we're working with or leading people who aren't like us. However, you are in control of how you show up each day. This book will help you mitigate bias and leverage your influence and personal leadership as you navigate uncertainty and change at work.

OTHER BIASES THAT IMPACT PERSONAL LEADERSHIP:

CONFIRMATIONAL BIAS: When we use our memory of past experiences to either support our existing beliefs or our prediction of future behaviours and situations. For example *The last time I hired a millennial they left in a year. That means if I employ another one they'll do the same thing.*

GROUP THINK: If you have a powerful leader, you'll see people gravitate to the group view rather than voice an opinion that might be contrary to that of everyone around you. If you are a Monty Python fan you will remember the scene in *The Life of Brian* – "You are all individuals", to which the crowd responds, "Yes we are all individuals".

Build your self-awareness muscle by understanding bias. It is an essential first step to deepening personal leadership.

FOUR

Unlocking possibility

'When you've exhausted all possibilities,
remember this: you haven't.'
—Thomas Edison

Before delving into the five stages of personal leadership development, it is important to first highlight why personal leadership matters and the subtleties of personal leadership distinctions that great leaders must work proactively to master. If you understand these subtleties, you are on your way to being the best leader you can be. This is where the art and science of leadership lays.

One of the greatest traps to unlocking what is truly possible for leaders is binary thinking, which is when a person believes that a decision has only two options available. For example, someone considering whether to change jobs will reflect on two options: I can stay and keep doing what I am doing or I can leave. *Binary thinking is the enemy of unlocked possibility. It stops us from considering many other options that may exist.*

In my executive coaching of leaders and facilitation of leadership teams, I constantly see and hear the traps of binary thinking. Binary thinking unveils itself in many different ways, and I believe it is sometimes exacerbated by leaders' technical backgrounds that can be black and white in their function. People leadership and leading yourself, however, are the opposite. They are grey and filled with opportunity, if explored fully.

Binary thinking can sound like this:

- 💡 I'm just a realist. This is how things really are. There's no point trying to resolve this. It is what it is.
- 💡 I really want to pursue my passion for running my own business but I don't have the money to leave my job yet so I'll just have to let that dream go.
- 💡 If I took that role and it didn't work out, I'd never get another job like the one I have now, so I'm best just to play it safe.
- 💡 I just don't have the charisma of other leaders. I'm too introverted.
- 💡 If I had more confidence, I'd have a go at that.
- 💡 There is no way I can trust them. They need to earn my trust first.
- 💡 I was just really honest. I told them exactly what I thought.

As you can see from the above statements, they are common and final in their expression. Any chance of growth, opportunity or possibility is shut down. Most people don't even realise they are being so definitive in blocking opportunity for themselves and others. They can draw on every example from the past to prove themselves right, yet they simultaneously lock their capacity and potential. When I ask them what they want, they can't articulate it. Instead, they'll answer my question with what they don't want. (That's okay—it's a start and it tells me there may be fear or lack of information).

In Buddhism, there is a concept of 'near enemies' and 'far enemies'. Far enemies are obvious enemies. For example, the far enemy of 'partnership' may be 'protection'. Near enemies, however, lurk in the shadows. They are the personal leadership distinctions that an abundant leader understands intuitively and practically. They sometimes appear to be positive, yet their impact can fall short of the mark.

Personal leadership distinctions

Some of the key leadership distinctions that have the most impact on organisations and the ability of leaders to connect and engage with others are as follows:

LOCKED POSSIBILITY Personal Leadership Immaturity	UNLOCKED POSSIBILITY Personal Leadership Intelligence
Pity	Compassion
Charisma	Congruence
Realist	Being present
Honesty	Transparency
Positive thinking	Reframed mindset
Attached	Committed
Confidence	Conviction
Trust earned	Trust given
Power over	Power with

Pity vs Compassion

On the surface, when pity shows up, it resembles compassion. They seem similar and are true near enemies of personal leadership intelligence. Pity can be condescending and a way of distancing yourself from another person. We feel 'bad' for someone else, while compassion is founded in dignity for another human being.

As a leader, if we 'pity' someone, we are supporting a position of superiority to the other human being. This is disempowering. I've seen this in my work with The Hunger Project, speaking to our country directors and discussing the impacts of westerners coming in to 'save Africa'. The trouble with this mindset is that it sets up superiority, and renders the people of Africa as being unable to solve their own problems. This is why I support of the methodology of The Hunger Project using appreciative inquiry to facilitate a mindset change. Never are the words 'donors' used in the work. We are partners in ending hunger together. Our mantra of 'seeing a billion people capable of ending their own hunger' is a stark contrast to 'seeing a billion people needing food'. Poverty is not about food, it's about lack of opportunity.

Compassion connects us to one another as human beings. While there are many definitions that exist that include the word 'pity' in the definition, in the context of this book I believe compassion is our ability to connect with another human and a motivation to do something to relieve their suffering. It isn't about fixing their problems for them, it's about holding the space for them to open up. Empathy can also be similar to pity when we 'feel with another person' to the point where we are also dragged down. This is why neuroscientists are currently exploring the difference that compassion makes.

Charisma vs Congruence

There is no doubt that, as human beings, we are drawn to charismatic people—especially in leadership. However, reliance on unsubstantiated charisma alone is a short-term strategy with damaging long-term implications. It can be as short lived as confidence.

There is more to leadership than charisma. Congruence wins every time because it builds trust. Leadership depth and substance come from congruence between the mind and the body, when what we say and do is in agreement with the values that matter most to us. Charisma is charm that inspires devotion, whereas congruence is about how we show up long term. In Amy Cuddy's book, *Presence* (2015) she talks about the fact that congruence is required for us to be able to trust and to build our ability to influence. Charisma can lead to group think, whereas a leader who is congruent has the wherewithal to set up bias mitigation strategies to counteract this positional power.

We know from a Neuroscience of Strategic Leadership perspective, that some gifted and charismatic leaders can *initially* have quite an influence over us. But, it is congruent leaders who are the ones that will make the long-term difference.

Realist vs Being Present

Being a realist is worn by many people like a badge of honour. The age old argument begins with whether you see yourself as an optimist or a pessimist. What all of these ignore is our need to connect as human beings. Facts alone will not guide you through your leadership. The ability to read the play and navigate the emotions that exist as a leader going through change, uncertainty and complexity requires leaders to be present in the moment.

Amy Cuddy states, "the lesson is that trust is the conduit of influence. And the only way to establish real trust is by being present". Realists are stuck in their existing paradigm. They shut down possibility.

Honesty vs Transparency

I remember being called into an organisation where two of the senior leaders had a huge blow up with one another. When I spoke to one of them, she stated very emphatically, "I just told them what I thought, I was honest". When I asked her, "Did you show care for the other person in the delivery of your honesty?" She had to admit that she didn't. The conversation was more focused on her venting her angst.

Honesty without care is poor leadership, and transparency will trump it every single time. Senior leaders know that when they're exposed to confidential information, honesty isn't always the best policy. I've coached leaders around this when I've heard them use statements like, *I was just being honest*. But the reality is that venting your spleen is not honesty, it's irresponsible, and discretion matters in these moments. When we dial up transparency with care, it quells threat within an organisation.

Positivity vs Reframed Mindset

Blind positive thinking is a delicate trap that can trip up all of us. When a colleague upsets you for example, you may think that moving to a 'positive mindset' will resolve the problem. However, positive thinking is not the same as a *reframed* mindset.

On its own, positive thinking can be infuriating; it is often used as a means of avoidance and not speaking up. It can become the crutch of a situation when you think resorting to this will shift a situation that needs positive action. For example, a coachee confided in me about being 'talked over', at work, regarding a project plan that they had made recommendations on and put together. The CEO decided to proceed an alternative way, and my coachee was convinced that letting the decision slide and then saving it for a later conversation was a 'positive mindset'.

The danger of a situation like this is that the conversation isn't being had with the person in question, and 'acceptance' is thought to be positive. When you supress your voice in this situation, the likelihood is that the issue will bubble up under the surface. Acceptance is okay as long as you are not remaining 'silent' about your own opinions and beliefs to appease someone else.

Mindset is not about blind positive thinking, it's about reframing your thoughts from unhelpful to helpful or resourceful. They imply action not silence and are focused on moving forward. Josie Thomson, one of my admired colleagues and friends, once said, 'You can't lie to your own brain'.

Leaders often suppress emotions such as anger and frustration because they're trying to be positive but positive thinking is the near enemy of a reframed mindset—it stops them from self-expressing and having a voice. Positivity or positive thinking alone does very little when trying to get a strategic plan or idea across the line. Suppression of emotion is like pushing a beach ball under water—there is only one way for that to go.

The notion of applying patience and a positive mindset is to not speak up or talk about the challenges with your CEO as demonstrated in the example above. In doing this you are stifling your own voice, which is completely disempowering. Instead of thinking you need to be patient, consider being curious. Have you ever discussed, with your CEO, how you can work together? If approached the right way, a dominant CEO will appreciate the direct conversation. For them to make a decision, what information do they need? How long do they take to decide? What patterns do you notice? If they are deliberative (focused on mitigating risk first), for example, you will never sell them an idea in one session. It can be frustrating to be the person strategically thinking this through. It is, however, a skill needed in managing up and saving time and angst long term.

Attached vs Committed

To build trust as a leader, you need to be capable of distinguishing attachment from commitment. Commitment is your willingness to give time and effort to something, whereas being 'attached' is a fixed state of being. It grips leaders in a way that cuts off insight, as they focus on things being the way they want them to be. As a result, decision making is difficult as things that can't be controlled are intertwined in the process; this makes life messy. When we are attached to an outcome or situation, our ability to lead and influence others is compromised. The lines become blurred on what is within our circle of control versus what is within our circle of concern.

Strong personal leadership is the ability to distinguish what's in our circle of control and our circle of concern, so we can let go of the things that we can't change. When we're attached to things in our circle of concern (not necessarily within our control), we're unable to progress. A good leader knows to focus on areas where they have control, or they have influence. They understand the difference between the two; like a retractable leash, they know when to pull the leash in and when to release control.

When Kenchamma, one of the elected panchayat leaders trained by The Hunger Project first arrived at her initial panchayat meeting, she was physically picked up by the male panchayat members and thrown out the door. They told her she could do her business from outside. If she were attached to her right to be operating from within that room, she would have lost control, but to stay committed to the things she could control and that mattered most to her and her community, she bravely sat at a table outside the council meeting room every day, and operated her business from there. By doing this, she brought electricity and water to her community. While nobody wants to see a woman treated in this manner and it angers you to think of a person being treated this way, her personal leadership enabled her to focus on what was in her control, to have the resilience to know where she could make a difference and how to navigate that well.

Letting go of attachment requires acceptance. As Michael J Fox says, "Acceptance doesn't mean resignation. It means understanding that something is what it is and there's got to be a way through it". When Nelson Mandela exited Robin Island prison he said, "As I walked out the door toward the gate that would lead to my freedom, I knew if I didn't leave my bitterness and hatred behind, I'd still be in prison". That's commitment.

Confidence vs Conviction

Be strong! Be confident! Ugh, you know the meme that shows up regularly on social media platforms. While it's nice to strive to be confident, the reality is, confidence is often a short-term feeling. The pressure to be confident in itself can create doubt. There are reams of articles on 'imposter syndrome' (the feeling that you are a fraud and will be found out any time soon); however, what is overlooked is that having some self-doubt is a good quality for a leader to have. On the flip side of this, overconfidence stops us from seeking insight to our blind spots and failings as leaders. Dan Gregory and Keiran Flanagan in Selfish, Scared and Stupid, highlight through Tomas Chamorro-Premuzic, a professor of business psychology at University College London, that lower confidence is in fact necessary for gaining competence.

A little self-doubt makes you question and get curious about people and situations. It is what helps people remain humble in positions of power. Conviction, on the other hand, is about being prepared and having evidence to support your beliefs, because you've explored your biases or blind spots. Conviction comes from taking action, competence, and knowing your stuff well enough that you can ask discovery questions that won't necessarily provoke you into threat response.

When faced with differences of opinion or changes that feel threatening, preparation is key to building conviction in what you do.

Trust Earned vs Trust Given

When we say that trust must be earned before it is given, we limit the capacity for meaningful connection and progress. Passive-aggressive stances like this statement shift us into a 'Mexican standoff' where no one moves forward and, as a result, distrust becomes stronger. We need to move to a state of trust, because trust changes our reality.

What if starting with trust created more trust? The challenge for leaders with this paradigm is that it requires them to shift their own behaviours by learning to set better boundaries with others and our time. When we begin with trust needing to be earned first, we are narrowing our view to a reality that is seen through fear and threat. This makes it difficult for us to open up our view. Judith E Glaser often speaks about "trust changing our reality". Strong personal leadership enables us to shift to a mindset of trust up front.

Power Over vs Power With

Power is a dynamic continually at play in the world of work. It's important to be able to differentiate between power to, power with, power over and power within.

I have witnessed leaders fail spectacularly when they have a mindset of entitlement around being respected for their role. Yes, there is a requirement for employees to behave in a certain way at work; however, they are under no obligation to respect you. When leaders lose control of their teams or colleagues and begin to exert 'power over' tactics, the result is always frustration, anger, more conflict, and turnover of roles.

Power over is about exerting our authority based on hierarchy within the organisation. It uses fear as a means to rule. Daniel Pink in *Drive* (2011) writes that human beings are motivated by three things: autonomy, mastery, and purpose. Today, where organisations are more flat, and we have higher proportions of contract workers, leaders need to be more proficient in generating buy-in of others, without relying on title. Power with is a concept that initially feels counter-intuitive to leaders who are used to a traditional hierarchical corporate model. When you have personal power within, you are no longer afraid to be curious or to ask questions to which you don't have the answers. As a result, you have conviction in your abilities to navigate those deeper, more complex conversations.

Power over others is a form of leadership driven from insecurity, ego and fear. In contrast, power with others comes from within. It means we can let go without necessarily losing control. When we rely on power that is based on position or job title, it stifles cultures, and it places teams into a threat response that inhibits everything from engagement, to performance, to innovation.

We know from a neuroscience perspective, that power over triggers threats in those around us, and it limits psychological safety within the workplace. As Eckhart Tolle wisely said, "Power over others is weakness disguised as strength".

PART 2

Navigating your way

Now that you have the foundations to unlock your leadership, it's time to move through the Step Up Ladder to set you up for success.

At the end of each chapter, I have listed questions to help you reflect on what you have learned and how it applies to your own leadership. *No matter where you work, taking the time to reflect is essential to personal leadership.* The sooner you begin to develop your own personal leadership, the more prepared you will be to advance in your career and be expansive in your impact on the world.

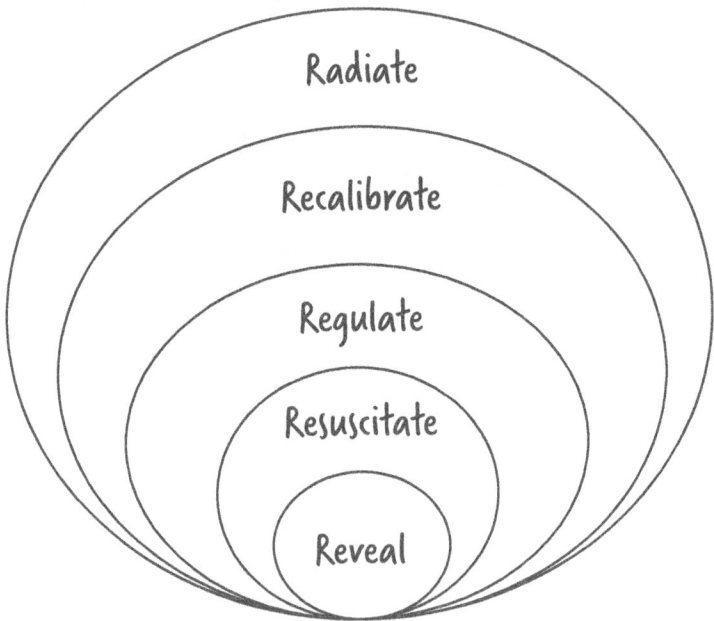

Figure 3: How to step up in your personal leadership

In Part 1, I outlined the art and science of why leading yourself first matters when moving from autopilot to aware to abundant. In Part 2, I will take you through the five steps to leveraging your full capacity as an abundant leader. The path is laid out in this book as follows:

1. **REVEAL:** This is about opening up and peeling back the layers. As autopilot is a state of non-consciousness, inevitably something happens or is 'revealed to us' alerting us to the fact that there is a need for change.

2. **RESUSCITATE:** Bringing your leadership back to life by getting in touch with the things that inspire you and fire you up. They are the essence of the contribution you are meant to make as a leader.

3. **REGULATE:** No one is perfect. Leadership is not perfect. It ebbs and flows and leading yourself means being aware of what you need to keep in check through regulating. Reactionary and emotionally explosive leaders create fear and often focus on the wrong things—the antithesis of a high performing work environment that requires psychological safety.

4. **RECALIBRATE:** Getting in touch with your intentions so you can leverage possibilities through change. Getting clear on this means you start to dampen ego-driven and fear-based behaviours. This skill is key to becoming an influential and strategic leader. It is also what truly opens up possibility. Trust and adaptability are key to recalibrating.

5. **RADIATE:** Finding the power within. When we have power within, we radiate in our leadership. We create an energy that others want to be around because we are congruent in the way we show up in mind and body.

As you move through the chapters in Part 2, you will gain insight to the 'state' you may be in at each stage, as well as the outcomes to aim for as you work through the book.

Personal leadership: The step-up ladder explained...

Focus	1. Assess: Where I may be at?
Reveal	Unconsciously incompetent: you may have blind spots or biases around your capability and capacity. At times, you may feel: • Lost • Confronted or confused • Busy 'on the treadmill' • Exhausted: busy 'on the treadmill' • Focus on external locus of control.
Resuscitate	Unconsciously incompetent moving to conscious incompetence: • Relief: 'it's not just me', followed by discomfort: tired but hopeful or determined to change • Small breakthroughs showing • Starting to be conscious of mind and body • Learning areas to work on to triage your personal leadership.
Regulate	Conscious incompetence moving to conscious competence: 'getting in the groove' • 2 steps forward 1 step back (feels like) • Faster recovery from setbacks • Becoming more aware of 'people pleasing' and 'perfectionism' • Decision making becoming more consistent.
Recalibrate	Conscious competence moving to unconscious competence: • Focusing on what is in my control and influence • Mentalising the impact of behaviours and likely responses of others before it occurs • Consistent practice of reflection and focus on what matters most.
Radiate	Unconscious competence without ego taking over: continuing to learn and grow: • Power within: conviction from preparation • People drawn to your inner light and presence • Conscious leadership • Feel lighter and calmer under pressure • Continued growth mindset to navigate change. Know when to dive back into 'resuscitate' when you get off course.

... Assess, Align and Action.

2. Align: Mind and Body	3. Action: Make progress
Before exploring your values, remember you are human. Use feedback to focus forward and align your mindset toward positive action and growth.	Adopt a mindset of abundance, possibility, and inclusion. Commit to being a better leader and doing the work, ensuring your tribe are there for support.
Develop, design, deliver and dream. Look within learning to tune in to your energy, creativity, vulnerability, and authenticity.	Invest in yourself. Improve yourself. Innovate the way you do things. Integrity at the core of everything you do.
Regulate your emotions, attention, and strengths.	Practice mindfulness: pay attention to your attention and intentions. Be responsive rather than reactive. Minimise technology distractions. Manage around weakness and invest in strengths.
Get clear on where you are heading: • Purpose: what are my intentions? • Perception: what is my impact? • Perspectives: are there other ways? • Possibility: take strategic action to move forward.	Understand and action change gaps between intentions and impact. Mentalise other people's perspectives. Learn from reality checks and mistakes. Focus on progress rather than perfection. Ability to adapt and pivot to grow influence as a leader.
Building trust and safety through consistency. Having powerful and transparent conversations with care. Congruence: presence is aligned in mind and body. Clear boundaries. Application of learnings across all stages so you can reapply and recalibrate continually.	Leveraged capacity through gratitude, grace, growth and gravitas—the rising tide that lifts all boats—focus on building capacity in others Regular focus on vitality, visual impression, verbal impact, visceral impact, and value delivered.

FIVE

Reveal: Peeling back the layers

Autopilot
Self-sabotage: when your behaviour may get in the way of your long-term goals. Unconscious incompetence moving to conscious incompetence.

Just reading the word 'reveal' can send many of us into a state of anxiety. Any personal leadership journey starts with a moment of 'revelation'. It can appear after:

- 360° feedback
- feedback in the moment (self-realisation)
- setback/failures
- running the treadmill of 'busy' when gaps/moments may reveal the need to change.

As human beings we are paradoxically complex and predictable at the same time. As a leader, the moment we become aware of our need to change—depending on our mindset—can be one of the greatest gifts. However, when we are wired towards the negative, initially the reveal stage can be challenging. For many people, they ruminate on 'what hasn't been right' for years. For others, it is that awful realisation experienced when we become *consciously incompetent*. This happens when we take a 'step up' into a new leadership role, and we have to let go of the 'old things' with which we felt so competent and familiar.

Feedback

Receiving feedback of any kind can be confronting. Before any change, there is a moment known as cognitive dissonance that produces a feeling of discomfort as a result of conflicting attitudes, beliefs, or behaviour. For example, a leader may believe they are great at building work relationships, yet suddenly an exit interview may reveal that, in fact, they are not doing it that well. In that moment, to restore balance and to reduce discomfort they will either take action to create change or they may convince themselves that the person doing the exit interview had no idea what they were talking about. As this scene from *Shrek* reminds us, it can be confronting to 'peel back the layers'.

Shrek: Ogres are like onions.

Donkey: They stink?

Shrek: Yes. No.

Donkey: Oh, they make you cry.

Shrek: No.

Donkey: Oh, you leave 'em out in the sun, they get all brown, start sproutin' little white hairs.

Shrek: No. Layers. Onions have layers. Ogres have layers. Onions have layers. You get it? We both have layers.

Donkey: Oh, you both have layers. Oh. You know, not everybody likes onions.

Mojo

When was the last time you truly felt joy at work? I once asked this question to a crowd and one of them replied, "joy's a pretty strong word. Couldn't you use a different word?". Wow. There was insight right in that moment, and they knew it as well.

It can be confronting to realise that maybe you are in a place where you never expected to be. Begin to pay attention to your mojo. Ask yourself these two questions:

1.   What energy do you bring as a leader?
2.   How are you currently showing up?

Mindset

The problem with peeling back the layers is it is one of the most challenging things for us to do as a leader and yet it is also one of the most liberating if we are committed to the process. As we explore the brain and what it means to be human, it can bring paradoxical emotion: an almost instant relief, *wow, it's not just me*, along with terror, *what does this mean now? How do I apply all this?*

Some leaders never take this first step. That is of course a choice, and it should lead to you questioning whether a leadership role is in your future regardless of the capacity in which that shows up (community, organisation etc.). Your mindset, as we know from Chapter 3, is the key to unlocking your capacity as a leader.

Your tribe

You don't have to do this all alone. Having an inner core of supporters, your 'tribe', is essential to encouraging and empowering us to be the very best we can be. So how do we know who belongs in our tribe and what qualities they should have?

During this stage, discretion and confidentiality is key. As you begin your personal leadership development, be clear on whom you trust to share information. They should be discreet and compassionate, your equals or above, those who are also committed to stretching you to reach your potential. There should also be clear boundary setting in your conversations. Clearly outline what is okay and not.

More importantly, it is not always responsible to share everything with those who report to you. They are looking up to you in your leadership, so while it is great to seek feedback on your leadership, it's not okay to overshare information. It will come back to bite you later. Be clear on the purpose of sharing information with your direct reports: is it to help them contribute to achieving something, or is it seeking sympathy and attention?

((·)) TUNE IN:

To your mindset:

Begin practicing the adoption of a growth mindset. Focus on the learnings and the process of growth.

To your tribe:

You don't have to go it alone. Find your tribe so you have a safe place to share setbacks as well as wins.

To feedback:

Learn to listen to feedback. If you don't have clarity on what change is needed, ask this question: What would I be doing differently in the future if I wanted to improve/perform well? The emphasis here is on behaviour; it needs to be actionable.

Note: Feedback should be a future-focused action. Ask for feedback, but ensure the question is focused on the future. For example, what three things would you like me to do differently in the future?

To your mojo:

How would you rate your energy levels on a scale of 1–10, with 10 being 'Yeah Baby!' (think Austin Powers). If your energy levels are low, it may be time to resuscitate your leadership.

📋 My self-assessment and actions

_____

_____

_____

_____

_____

_____

_____

_____

_____

_____

_____

_____

_____

_____

_____

_____

SIX

Resuscitate: Triage your leadership

'Do something your future
self will thank you for.'
—Heather Swan (World record holding extreme
sport athlete and wingsuit pilot)

Autopilot towards Aware
Self-conscious: when you become aware of
what others around you may think of you. It's a
sense of 'being watched'. Can lead to shyness or
introversion as awareness becomes heightened.
Unconscious incompetence moving
to conscious incompetence.

Resuscitate sounds kind of dramatic doesn't it? Just like the process of triage in an emergency ward of a hospital, resuscitating your leadership may be at different levels of severity. Personal leadership goes beyond your technical skill or knowledge.

More than ever, we need to breathe life back into the quality of leadership in our organisations. It's time to bring your authentic style of leadership to the forefront. Before you start leading others, you first need to explore deep within yourself. Becoming a self-expressed, strong leader requires deep self-awareness and the courage to confront it. Find *your* voice. Find *your* leadership character, and discover the legacy you want to leave behind.

Such personal growth can overwhelm us and if comparison kicks in, we are left feeling insecure and disempowered. Finding the leader that sits within us requires us to resuscitate the heart and humanity of our leadership. Everyone can find a way to lead when they know how. When we bring ourselves to life, we preserve the integrity of our values; we invest in our talents; we improve and learn; and we innovate.

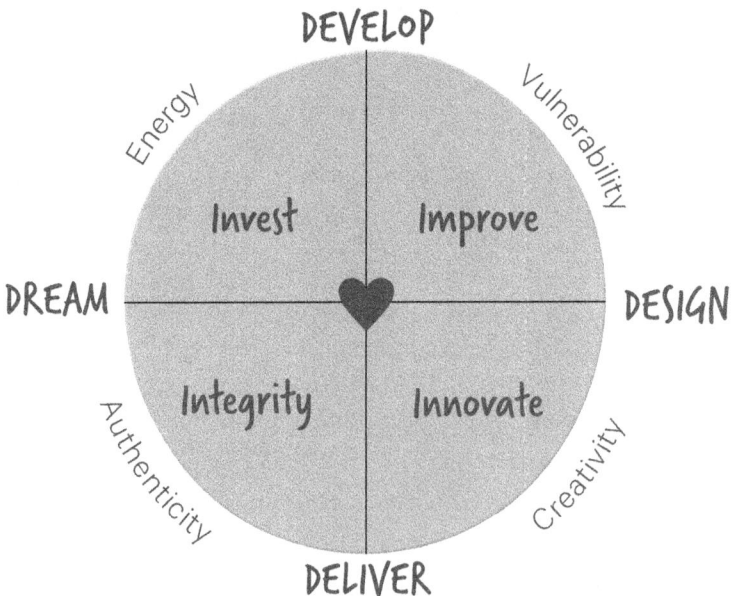

Figure 4: Resuscitate your leadership

DEVELOP

When a leader believes they are too old to learn, can't learn something new, or frankly, just can't be bothered, then company culture and performance will stagnate or decline. Too often, an executive leadership team will argue and fight, and cling to command and control leadership styles that won't survive the future of work. Many people want to be better leaders, but their organisations don't provide the training and support they need to be at their best. Resuscitating your leadership starts with accepting that personal and professional development is an ongoing learning process—mastery comes with effort and consistency.

I worked with a client who, prior to our coaching session, read Janine Garner's book, *It's Who You Know* (2017). The book allowed her to see the gaps in her networking capabilities. She was suddenly in a position where she could choose to feel bad about her lost opportunities, or she could act, deliver, and be a role model for others. Her success has come from developing and investing in herself, rather than staying focused on what 'she didn't do earlier'. It's okay to stand at the door and see the errors of the past, but don't stay standing at the door for too long. Move forward and continue to focus on growth.

DESIGN

There is no 'one way' to do things as a leader. Designing your leadership is an art where you will improve along the way as you find what works for you. Take the elements of others' leadership that you admire but don't be afraid to find your personal stamp too. And remember that you don't have to go it alone—partner with people who complement you. We achieve so much more when we work as a collective.

DELIVER

Actions speak louder than words. Resuscitating your leadership requires action: one step of meaningful progress at a time is what helps you move forward in a positive way. If you aren't walking your talk and adhering to the values you hold dear, others are unlikely to follow. We know that talk is cheap and by taking deliberate action to becoming a better leader, you naturally build confidence. You can't expect others to follow if you aren't delivering on your promises to yourself and others.

DREAM

We've forgotten to dream. It's not necessarily intentional; however, the influx of information today is overwhelming to us all. We're stuck in the frenetic pace of 'busyness', and when we wear it like a badge of honour, it can be difficult to pull ourselves out of the rut. Personal leadership is about being true to what matters to you, your vision and your dream of a better future for yourself. The minute we stifle our dreams and tell ourselves, *it's just how it is*, we've slotted ourselves into a state of procrastination and victim-hood. Yes, there may be sacrifices along the way, and it may take longer than anticipated to achieve something, but never lose your commitment to fulfilling the things that give you a sense of purpose—the things that energise you and make you feel alive.

INVEST in yourself

There is no glory in neglecting yourself. No heroism in being the person 'who works the longest hours in the office'. You cannot lead others if you neglect your own health and wellbeing.

Energy

Judith E. Glaser says the energy of a leader makes or breaks trust, and essentially the psychological safety of an organisation. The energy you bring to the table, as a leader, is proportionate to your use of your natural talents. We often see leaders on a treadmill of work and busyness. They have a sense of discontent but aren't sure what it is. When leaders don't apply their natural talents to their daily tasks they feel unfulfilled and lost, and may find it difficult to focus or take action. Gallup Strengths often help my coachees reveal what energises them. By identifying what is missing, it enables them to take action by finding ways to use these talents.

For example, I worked with a coachee who had strong influence themes in her top five strengths; however, she wasn't putting her influence to use in the area where she felt most passionate. She was in a high compliance, sustainability and environment role, yet her work in compliance wasn't necessarily suited to her talents. Her talents were more aligned with bringing about influence and change. This session shifted her thoughts about how she could redirect her career in the future to still lead within the area she was passionate about (sustainability and environment), by adapting her focus to look for opportunities to move into roles that had a stronger focus on influence and communication.

((ψ)) TUNE IN: Your energy matters

Do you pay attention to your energy levels? The energy you bring to the table, as a leader, is proportionate to your investment in refuelling. When you aren't conscious to your mojo or energy, you are more likely to find yourself on the treadmill of discontent.

Are you investing in your talents? Have you completed a Gallup Strengths top five report for example or the VIA strengths equivalent?

What is your strategy for self-care? For example, are your periods of leave throughout the year scheduled in advance?

Are you regularly investing in your personal and professional development?

IMPROVE yourself

Personal leadership requires a mindset of lifelong learning and growth. More than ever, we need leaders who take responsibility to learn, grow, and improve, so they can foster psychological safety for high performance. Our curiosity about others is just as relevant to ourselves.

Where are our capability gaps? Is the challenge a capacity issue? When we look at this, we can identify the areas in which we need to improve, so we can learn, grow, and become better leaders.

Vulnerability

If there were one book that all leaders should read as they explore their personal leadership, it would be *Daring Greatly* by Brene Brown

(2015). Her definition of vulnerability involves being truly seen, having the courage to be imperfect, having the compassion to treat ourselves kindly and connecting with others by being authentic. The Macquarie Dictionary (2018) definines vulnerability as 'susceptible to being wounded' and 'liable to physical hurt'.

Vulnerability in the context of personal leadership is about being enough and getting on with the job of leadership and letting go of our need to control everything. It is the foundation of developing an abundant mindset, accepting that you will make mistakes, and that you will need to draw on all your courage to make the tough decisions. "We love seeing the raw truth and openness in other people, but we're afraid to let them see it in us". Leaders for the 21st century are facing uncertainty regularly and, as a result, the need to be perfect or to be 'people pleasers' will serve no one. Especially ourselves.

TUNE IN: Your vulnerability matters

Leaders are lifelong learners. What are you doing to continually learn, grow, and improve?

Are you being 'seen'?

How is perfectionism and 'people pleasing' showing up in your leadership?

When has this held back your leadership?

How are you celebrating the successes of yourself and/or your team?

What role does gratitude play in your life and leadership?

Are you able to admit when you're wrong? Or are you covering up your mistakes and blaming others. Leaders stepping up take responsibility for their actions.

INNOVATE the way you do things

As leaders in the fourth stage of resuscitating leadership, we need to make things happen; we need to influence; we need to build relationships; and we need to think strategically. When we innovate, we become comfortable with experimenting and exploring ways that work for others and ourselves. We want to adapt, but not necessarily copy. We might be curious about others' leadership style. The key though is not to pretend to be someone else or you'll end up like David Brent from *The Office*. By adapting you can expand your leadership arsenary and continually reinvent the way you work. When we reflect on our strengths and our ability to execute, to influence, to build relationships, and to think strategically, we may question our lesser talents.

During another coaching session, and again, reviewing the Gallup Strength's assessment, my coachee discovered she had no strategic thinking talent themes in her profile. This didn't mean she couldn't be strategic but it did indicate that her way of being strategic was *through* relationships. This enabled her to excel in her role as a leader, and helped her revitalise and resuscitate her personal leadership.

Creativity

As we outlined in Part 1, binary thinking is the enemy of possibility. Creativity is key to unlocking possibility and moving through problems that are new or complex. Often our ideas are mediocre, not because we don't have the creative thinking ability, but because we haven't persisted in exploring more options. Our fixed mindset kicks in as we realise coming up with creative options takes effort. It can be challenging. If we remain in a fixed mindset, it's likely that we will give up early and more often than not, limit our creative ideas.

Northwestern University researchers Brian Lucas and Loran Nordgren completed a study with students to see the number of ideas they could come up with for things to eat and drink at Thanksgiving dinner. They were given ten minutes, and were then given a short break before being given an additional ten minutes to generate more ideas. They discovered that generating ideas is hard and this makes us doubt ourselves; therefore, we often decrease our expectations about how we will perform. Follow-up studies also showed that we interpret the feeling of difficulty incorrectly, often giving up because we think we aren't creative.

I've also seen this in group situations where I have asked executives to work in teams to establish understanding of their colleagues and what 'success' looks like to them. What often happens is that the conversations stop short because they are asking closed questions or aren't sure what questions to ask. In our busy worlds, we've lost the art of listening and asking great questions. Our curiosity is hampered.

Like any change that is usually preceded by cognitive dissonance, our creativity can be the same. Before our great ideas, there is likely to be a feeling of frustration or a desire to just give up. In generating new ideas for doing things differently, be persistent in your search of options. Is there another way? What works for me? Who can help me? Who does this well? What can I learn from them? Mitigate the frustration by thinking about the great questions to ask earlier in the process. You never know what you might discover. (Jacobs, 2016)

(((↯))) TUNE IN:

Your creativity matters

Are you willing to experiment with new ways of doing things in a way that works for you?

Do you partner up with those who have complementary skills and knowledge to your own?

When did you last look to unexpected places for new ideas and ways of doing things?

INTEGRITY at the core of everything you do

'When your values are clear to you,
making decisions becomes easier'.
—Roy E. Disney

Seems so obvious to expect integrity at the core of everything you do as a leader. However, because our non-conscious system runs so fast, often we aren't equipped to make wise decisions if we haven't invested in getting clear on our core values.

Your personal values are your preferences, the things that matter most, and the things that take priority. Being clear on your core values (the 'non-negotiables') is critical to leading a life where your actions are aligned with what matters most. Just like an anchor in rough seas, clarity of your values enables you to live a life that can weather the storms that come with being a leader.

Our ability to make wise decisions can be swayed more easily if we don't have clarity on our core values. Remaining in integrity with your values takes courage. Without it, internal and external conflict and inconsistent decision making can take hold and create stress.

In *Great by Choice* (2011), Jim Collins and Morten T Hanson said, "we've found in all our research studies that the signature of mediocrity is not an unwillingness to change; the signature of mediocrity is chronic inconsistency'. Fear rules us when our values are not clear; we weaken accordingly as we lose our power from within. It leaves us vulnerable to conformity due to the power of group-think and our deep-seated need to belong.

Authenticity

Authenticity does not mean 'being yourself' at the cost of everything and everyone else. It requires transparency in your dealings while showing care for yourself and others. It is genuine, not manipulated and grounded in trustworthiness.

As you explore authenticity, reflect on your positioning—your unique DNA code that makes different to others. This is made up of your values, your experiences, accomplishments, and knowledge as well as your talents. It also includes your goals or future aspirations. Authenticity is not a static state. It is an evolving state that allows you to grow while removing the elements that no longer serve you well.

The roadmap to authenticity is about bringing your values to life in the way you live each day. This clarity is the foundation to being strategic with stakeholders, becoming clear on what you want to be known for and developing the gravitas and presence required to be an expansive and abundant leader. Taking a bold stand for what you believe in is a key part of influence and persuasion as a leader.

(((Y))) TUNE IN: Your authenticity matters

Are you clear on your core values?

When did you last assess your values?

How are you living your core values?

Are you consistent in the way you lead?

On a scale of 1–10, how comfortable are you speaking and acting with integrity in tough situations, with 10 being *I'm excellent at it*. Can you remember examples to support your rating?

My self-assessment and actions

_____

_____

_____

_____

_____

_____

_____

_____

_____

_____

_____

_____

_____

_____

_____

_____

SEVEN

Regulate: The ebb and flow of leadership

'The secret of change is to focus all of your energy, not on fighting the old, but on building the new.'

—Socrates

Aware
Self-aware: knowing one's internal states,
preference, resources and intuitions (definition
by Daniel Goleman in Emotional Intelligence).
Conscious incompetence and conscious
competence (leaning closer to competence).

There is no such thing as a perfect leader. Even in a state of awareness, it is impossible to know everything. Every one of us, no matter how progressive we are, has ebbs and flows in their leadership. The ability to find your flow through the art of regulating yourself allows you to tap into your own wisdom and willingness to be a better leader.

In dealing with stress, adversity, and set-backs our ability to draw on our strengths, remain grounded, grow, and thrive over time is impacted by our ability to adapt to change while remaining true to our values. Our ability to rebound from adversity can be developed and learned both at an individual, team, community, and organisational level by addressing the way we think, feel, and behave when working through change.

Many scenarios can trigger a threat response in you as a leader. The future of work is guaranteed to challenge you. With more than five generations in the workplace, the rise of the freelancers and contract workers as well as the epic rate of technological change will all work to push you into the unknown on many levels. An example may be introducing flexibility into an organisation for the first time. This can trigger a threat response in some leaders depending on their capacity for stress, experiences from the past, and their beliefs.

Within our workplaces there are numerous 'unwritten rules' by which we expect people to abide. Unwritten rules are the rules that exist in an organisation, even though they aren't formulated in a policy on paper. You notice them when you start somewhere new: *this is how we do things here* or *I wouldn't do that if I were you, that's a sure-fire way to see your career go backwards*. The unwritten rule of a 'face time' culture is an inherent, often unspoken belief held by many leaders, which is that to perform a role well, employees should be sitting at their desk, working more than eight hours a day. It could be predicated on the notion that if you can't be seen, then you potentially you can't be trusted.

This initial threat reaction within us is potentially a limbic or emotional response from the hippocampus or our 'library' of past situations, events or other people's stories. Maybe we experienced distrust of someone who worked from home and now our belief is that all employees need close supervision? The prefrontal cortex is connected to this limbic system, and it has the power to override the fast or reflexive system (also known as our X system). Hardwired responses that are characterised by their sensory and automatic nature can impede our abilities to lead ourselves and others.

If an employee wants a flexible work environment, you will need to regulate your first reaction that may be the 'threat' of not trusting someone working 'out of sight' based on your own need for certainty. If you can recognise this predisposition, then you are more likely to generate a new belief instead, which in turn can create new wiring in your brain. It can also prompt you to step up in your own leadership. Are you focused on outcomes, or focused on people doing things *the way you like them to be done.*

For example, you may decide to regulate your initial thoughts to the following new thought: *My team is outcome-focused, and I hold them accountable; therefore, how they get their work done is potentially not as important as the outcome itself.* Our C system or reflective system is governed by the prefrontal cortex, and is often called the 'new brain'. It is slower, controlled, intentional, and can regulate our prepotent responses. Our reflective system is one that helps us make wiser decisions, inhibiting those that are driven by threat or our 'fight and flight' reaction.

If we know that the prefrontal cortex can override our X system and create new wiring through neuroplasticity, then we know we can train willing leaders to regulate their behaviour to demonstrate the traits of courage, humility, accountability, and empowerment. All of which are essential to strong personal leadership. It is also essential for leaders to understand the basic wiring of their brain and its love of habit and focus toward safety and efficiency. Understanding this preference and using the tools in this book will help you to appreciate other people's perspectives and new ideas, allowing you to work in a much more inclusive way.

The other element to regulating yourself is developing your self-awareness. To regulate bias, thoughts, and feelings, leaders need to understand the things that trigger them (and those around them) into a threat response that shows up as fight, flight, freezing or appeasing. Some of the following may trigger us into 'threat':

- ☀ Fear
- ☀ Lack of knowledge or information about a situation or person
- ☀ A feeling of uncertainty
- ☀ Feedback
- ☀ Positional conversations where both parties believe they are right
- ☀ Effort, challenge: being pushed out of your comfort zone on highly complex issues
- ☀ Comparison: seeing others' success as a threat to our own success.

When you can identify what triggers you into a threat response, you can develop strategies for regulating your own behaviour. In this chapter, we will talk about regulating emotions, attention, and strengths all of which impact our ability to be responsive rather than highly reactive.

Emotions

If we are in touch with our own emotional state, we are better prepared to ensure our focus is in the right place, that we are forging social connections needed to thrive, and that we can regulate our emotions when under pressure. Leaders and managers who are committed to an outcome and are focused on what is within their control or influence are better placed to make tough decisions in a complex world.

When faced with change, complexity or setbacks leaders often struggle to accept the reality of what is occurring. They will pretend 'not to know' or miss the central premise of what is occurring to stay 'safe' or to avoid a tough decision. This is when critical business and people decisions can be hampered. Our brain's default response is habit; we like to avoid change and remain comfortable. This can lead to denial. Yet, as Seth Godin says, "safe is now the new risky," in a world that is complex and changing rapidly. Resilient leaders can recognise this resistance within themselves and can regulate their emotions to move into clearer, rational thinking.

Tune into your emotions: label them

Emotions left unattended eventually rise to the surface and create explosive and reactive leaders. It's like tuning into a radio station, if isn't tuned on the mark, it's just background noise. Neuroplasticity is the ability of the brain to change itself as needed so it can perform more efficiently and can show up as a changing of the strength of neuron connections, or by adding new cells. Jeffrey Schwartz, co-author of *You are not your brain* (2016) writes about the power of labeling emotions and how that can help us move from the limbic system of the brain into the prefrontal cortex. In my coaching (and if I am honest, even in my own language preferences) coachees say, *I think, I think*, whenever I ask them how they feel about something. Coachees may skirt around issues with details. Often, questions need to be repeated because they're not listening to the question; they are focused on the inner world within their own head. When people don't label an emotion, the situation remains in conflict within their own mind. This impacts their ability to lead others because people sense the internal chaos occurring for you. Their focus is scattered.

Further to this, ensuring that we don't suppress our emotions is an essential part of managing our stress, as suppression can lead to dire results. Labeling emotions also ensures that 'what we resist doesn't persist' and helps regulate emotional triggers and move us forward.

Tap into your intuition

For a variety of reasons, there is a belief that in organisations emotion should not play a role in decision-making. Contrary to this belief, emotion, when regulated, can play a pivotal role in leaders being able to make great decisions. For example, a leadership team may have to make a decision regarding manufacturing of clothing in a developing country. The decision to manufacture there may make sense financially and legally; however, if there is a gut feeling amongst the executive team that it isn't in line with the company's values, they may decide to dig deeper into the workplace practices of the overseas manufacturer before committing to moving ahead. This is an example of where the combination of logical and emotional decision making is critical.

The same use of intuition is also important in our own personal leadership. What is my intuition telling me to explore or question? Do I have biases or beliefs that trigger me into threat? Am I able to differentiate between my intuition and biases?

Manage expectations

Expectation management is also critical to managing emotions. As David Rock said, "What you expect is what you experience". Do you enter situations with others already expecting them to react or behave in a certain way? Does this lead you to make assumptions that potentially aren't valid? Expectations may also impact leadership when leaders who overpromise and under-deliver trigger a threat response in their employees that curtails performance.

The primary organising principle of the brain is to mitigate threat. As a result, when setting clear expectations with others, some leaders may avoid the hard tasks for fear of rejection or hurting someone's feelings. If we learn how to regulate our emotions, we have the capacity to improve our compassion and regulate any potential emotional spikes that occur when dealing with difficult or challenging employees. We can do this by practising techniques that consciously help engage the prefrontal cortex, such as reappraisal of situations, reconsolidating fear memories so they can be remembered and reframed, mindfulness, and erring on the side of caution when managing expectations and setting goals so we don't make promises we can't keep.

If you take into consideration these insights and learnings, the regulation of emotions at work is critical to building a high performing culture. Two steps to achieving this are to educate and train leaders on how to manage emotion at work, and to review the overall cultural practices of the organisation so that strategies that minimise threat and enhance performance can be developed.

To be proficient at making things happen, influencing stakeholders, building relationships and thinking strategically leaders need to be equipped with the knowledge and skills of regulating emotions using neuroscience. If you have leaders with the resilience and capability to manage emotions at work (their own and those of their employees), then you are on your way to creating a better organisational culture.

(((ᶦᴵ))) TUNE IN: TO YOUR EMOTIONS

Start to pay attention to your feelings. Label the feeling: what is it? A feeling is a feeling, it isn't a fact. Labelling helps quell the threat response in the brain.

Our initial bio-chemical reaction to events and conversations isn't something we can control. However, we can control what we do with the thoughts and feelings that arise. Respond wisely, and if emotions are heightened use the 24hr rule—sleep on it before taking any action.

Don't send emails when angry. This seems obvious; however, I am stunned at how many people continue to do this at senior levels.

Attention

Never, in our history, have we had a crisis of attention like we do today. The impact of technology has been forecast for a long time. I remember being a graduate at News Limited and learning about the impact the internet would have on our classifieds business back in the early 90s, and it is fascinating to see the changes that have occurred since I was a junior marketing graduate running around the halls of the newspaper building in Bowen Hills. Everything we predicted, well and truly, happened within less than 20 years.

Linda Stone, who worked at IBM and Apple in the 1990s recognised that the evolution of technology would impact our attention. She coined the phrase *Continual Partial Attention* in 1998, which is the process of paying simultaneous attention to a number of sources of incoming information, but at a superficial level. We are paying attention, but only partially.

Arianna Huffington in her book *Thrive* (2015) also reveals that smart phone users are checking their devices every six and a half minutes, which equates to more than 150 times per day. Also that 28 percent of our time is dealing with emails, the equivalent of more than 11 hours per week.

Mindfulness practices that involve the mental discipline of training where our attention goes, are important for empowering leaders to manage discomfort, stress, and change over time. The ability to regulate attention through mindfulness practices has shown to improve wellbeing by reducing burnout, the ability to demonstrate compassion, and becoming conscious of our own emotional stability.

Pay attention to your attention and intentions

Our head goes where we focus. If we aren't checking in on where our attention is, then the reality is that we are a little like a drunk driver. You think you are in control, you take short cuts assuming you will evade detection and you believe you can pull off looking sober—most likely you will be busted. Our attempts to hide technology when in meetings or conversation is exactly the same.

Some leaders believe that *multi-tasking is a great talent that improves the speed and productivity of work*. The impact of divided attention is significant and has been proven to decrease high performance. An example of this is the case study regarding mobile phone technology on the likelihood of having a car accident. It has been proven that in the five minutes following a phone call a person is four times more likely to have an accident. This 'crack in consciousness' known as the 'attentional blink', highlights how mindfulness and being present has benefits that far outweigh the detrimental impacts of switching and divided attention that occur when multi-tasking (McEvoy, et al., 2007).

I see distraction most often in how people *transition* from meeting to meeting. Usually in the first ten minutes you can tell that they aren't present. Their head is still mulling over the details of whatever it was they were doing before they walked in the door. They're missing what's happening now. No wonder we continually hear poor communication at work. The second is paying attention to your intentions. Too often we make decisions based on an intent that isn't grounded in it's focus. It's blurred with pride, ego, and entitlement. This isn't a situation for just the 'bad guys', it is a fundamental part of being human. Many leaders strike issues when they have no clarity on what their intentions are to begin with.

If we are to 'read the play' as leaders we need insight, that combination of intuition and deliberate reflection that helps guide us to make better decisions and to build connection with others. Without it, trust is near impossible and organisation cultures begin to lull into a false sense of security that comes from being 'busy' rather than 'productive'.

Get present in the moment

Sawubona translated means *I see you*. It is a common greeting in northern Natal tribes in Africa and is a powerful demonstration of being present in the moment with others. How many people truly listen to you? How good does it feel to be truly heard by another human being? Remember to take a breath and pause to get present in the moment. You never know what you might 'see'. Becoming conscious of where your focus is, and gently bringing it back to the present, allows you to become conscious of your mindset. For example, are you tapping into a mindset of abundance? Is a scarcity mindset showing up without you realising?

((ᵠ)) TUNE IN: To YOUR ATTENTION

There are two questions leaders need to ask themselves regularly:

1. Where is my attention?

2. What are my intentions?

Note: As human beings, we have a negative bias. If you flipped to a reframed mindset focused on what is possible, how might you see the world differently? Just the introduction of the questions above is a huge leap forward to being more mindful in your leadership.

Strengths and shadows

As a Gallup Strengths Certified Coach, I have taken hundreds of people through their strengths profile. The Gallup Strengths tool measures your talent, which is different to your knowledge and skills, acquired over your life and career. The key premise of strengths is that talents—our natural way to think, feel, and behave—become strengths when we invest in them and learn to use them productively. Gallup use the analogy of 'balcony' and 'basement' in reference to knowing when to dial your themes up and when to dial them down—when is your strength helping you, when is it working against you?

Personally, I prefer the reference to strengths having shadows. How long is the shadow cast by your strengths? Even if you aren't aware of your themes, think about the things that make you great. These will, at times, present themselves as your greatest weakness. The key here is to develop and invest in your talents so they underpin your position as a leader worth following. Your strengths can play a role in shaping your emotions, so be wise to their impact on yourself and others. Like a pencil, if it's not regularly sharpened it can become blunt, smudgy, or not used at all.

For example, I have *activator* high in my themes, which means *let's get started*. I create momentum. When I'm not using this theme well it shows up as follows:

- 💡 Taking on commitments too quickly and then having to back-pedal to make them work because I haven't considered my existing commitments
- 💡 Not closing out something that I started. I'm already off and focused on the next new shiny thing.

You can imagine how difficult writing a book is for me. Luckily I have other talent themes at play that help me override and manage around the above weaknesses. Here is another example:

Jack has presence. He can take control of situations and make decisions. He doesn't shy away from conflict or confrontation. He is direct and decisive and can be persuasive, compelling others to follow. However, lately in meetings his colleagues describe him as opinionated, inflexible, bossy, controlling, and rude at times-a know it all.

How can Jack be more productive and reduce the shadow of his strength? Perhaps he can let situations unfold without always feeling the need to step in. He might consciously ask for the opinions of others, take time to listen and reflect on how he responds to conflict and disagreements. Building awareness of how his direct style can land with his audience may help him build empathy and be aware that others may view situations through a different filter.

When you know how to navigate the shadows and weaknesses you cast through self-awareness, you can bring light to your leadership, and your journey becomes easier. Your strengths are also the clue to what energises you, as we discovered in Chapter 6. Knowing this allows you to make good decisions. If you know your strength is to learn new things and try innovative new ways of doing things, then a career progression into a space that is steady and routine is unlikely to fire you up. When we aren't energised, we tend to move back down the ladder into the self-sabotage space. The exception to this is when we take action knowing there is something not quite right for us.

The other element of regulating our strengths is becoming aware of how others may see our strengths as weaknesses. When people sense you are different, you may need to consider this so you can manage perceptions and find ways to communicate with them so they understand you better. This component of designing around your weakness allows you to manage perceptions, to find ways that work for you, and to minimise the friction that might get in the way of how you lead and motivate yourself. This is also the clue to forming strategic and complementary partnerships using the following process:

How do I manage around my weaknesses?	1st Question to Ask: Does this weakness stop me achieving what I need to do? If No then don't worry about it anyway! If YES then Innovate or Partner Up:
	INNOVATE: What strengths do I have that will help me achieve what I need to do?
	PARTNER UP Who is great at this and can complement my strengths?

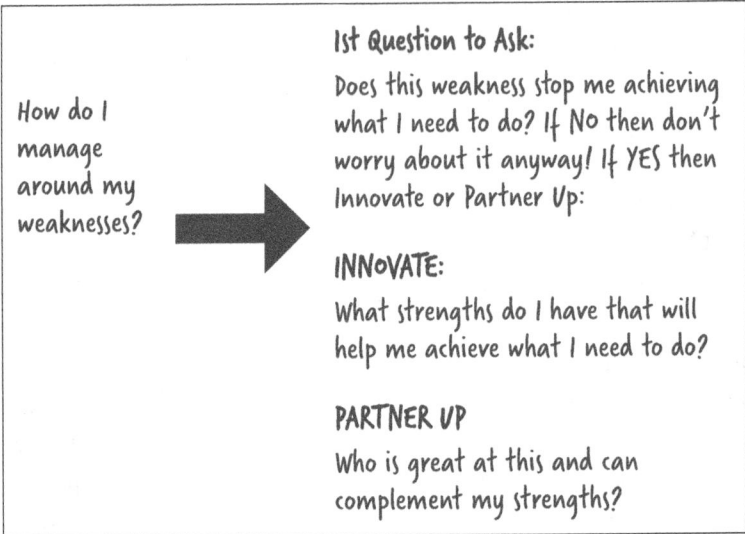

The Gallup Strengths tool also uses a framework known as the Leadership Domain Model. In essence, this framework highlights your preferences as a leader to be Executing, Influencing, Relationship Building or Strategic Thinking in your approach to leadership. Of course, all leaders need to do all four things. The opportunity with regulating your strengths is to reflect on how you might use your talent themes to deal with situations, people or decisions.

Asking yourself the question, *what needs to be achieved?* may help in regulating your strengths so you can consider whether it is about making things happen, speaking out as an influencer, building a stronger team/relationships or mapping out the strategic possibilities to move forward. This simple question enables you to interrupt your default patterns of behaviour and to think about how you may approach situations or people based on what is most likely to work for you and the person involved.

((|)) TUNE IN: TO YOUR TALENT THEMES OR STRENGTHS

Do you know your talents? If you don't, you can take the Gallup Strengths assessment here: https://www.gallupstrengthscenter. com/

What strengths do others see in you? If you aren't sure, ask some people who work closely with you. What are the top three strengths they see in your leadership?

How might your strengths sometimes be your greatest weakness if not used productively?

TIP: If you asked people for feedback on your strengths, remember to thank them. Acknowledge why it matters to you, and express gratitude for their time. Acknowledging the relationship is an important part of influence.

When you reflect on the past six months, when have you felt most energised? What were you doing? This may be a clue to your natural talents or strengths.

Knowing your talents, if you invested in them by using them productively, how might those strengths make you a better leader?

((I)) TUNE IN:

To your emotions:

Learn to label your feelings. Calling them out helps quell threat in the brain so you can respond more consciously.

Practice mindfulness or meditation to calm your brain's deceptive messages.

To your attention:

Pay attention to your attention and intentions. Where the brain goes the body follows. Gently guide yourself back to the present when you catch yourself being distracted.

When in a meeting, remove your phone from the table/your pocket or turn it off.

To your strengths:

Become clear on your talents. Complete your Gallup Strengths Top 5 assessment at www.gallupstrengthscenter.com to discover how to use your talents wisely. Understand how they may sometimes present as weakness if not regulated.

My self-assessment and actions

_____

_____

_____

_____

_____

_____

_____

_____

_____

_____

_____

_____

_____

_____

_____

EIGHT

Recalibrate: Leverage possibility through change, uncertainty, and complexity

Aware moving to Abundant
Self-leadership: having a developed sense of who you are, what you can do, and where you are going coupled with the ability to influence your communication, emotions, and behaviours on the way to getting there. (Definition by Bryant and Kazan in Self Leadership (2012). Conscious competence moving to unconscious competence.

Recently, I was coaching a CEO who was having issues with perception of his leadership. He was frustrated with the process because, in his eyes, he was a pragmatic leader: focused on making things happen and ensuring his company upheld the highest standards and met all the compliance requirements that go with an organisation of its scale and responsibility. What he wasn't aware of, though, was the impact that he was having on others when in meetings. People watched his body language. Whenever a potentially controversial conversation struck, people would look for his reactions.

When we started working together, we became focused on where his intentions were in those moments and in those meetings when he was asking questions and interacting with colleagues. It was then that he realised that his intention with the questions he asked was actually to reveal the weakness of a person's argument and take them down in the process. It was steeped in judgment and shaming of the other person who potentially hadn't prepared as much as they should have or who didn't have access to full information. He could see the gaps in their arguments. However, in organising and discussing his approaches, he became aware that his intention was to bring reputational damage to the person involved. When he became attuned to this, he saw the impact that was having on others. It was encouraging others to exhibit these behaviours and inevitably bring on corridor conversations' post-meeting that continued in this manner. This insight was exactly what he needed in order to reframe the way he led and it opened him up to new approaches to situations—in the way a true 'leader' would act.

Authentic personal leaders continually recalibrate; they're always asking, *What's my intention?* before they act. Intentions direct exactly where your attention goes. Like a GPS voice recalculating the destination, leaders also need to recalibrate so that they can unlock possibility and look at ways of being far more strategic in creating these new possibilities.

This particular leader has eliminated his original persona from his leadership style. This has had a huge impact on how he has been perceived, on the progress he's making in his career, and his ability to connect with people in ways that no longer means his is entrenched in water-cooler conversations about what's going on in the organisation and what's not right with it.

His ability to see what is going on through regulating his emotions and recalibrating and being clear on outcome has kept him focused on purpose. His ability to do this has meant he can see the change gaps required in his leadership, and he's taking the reality checks required to navigate forward as a leader in his organisation.

Let's take a look at the process of recalibration.

Building trust

Trust is as the foundation of recalibration. Without trust, we can't move into a co-creating space where the brain is willing to partner with others. When we're in a state of distrust, we become resistant and emotional, and we operate from the limbic part of the brain.

We know that emotions enhance memory, which can work both ways for leaders. Past experiences that are confronting or painful, can trigger responses to events based on confirmational bias, which can lead to potentially poor judgement and outcomes, while positive experiences can motivate and engage us by appealing to our emotions and memory. Leaders who understand that our social brain default (when the brain is not activated or doing anything) is to think about the self, about others' thoughts and about others' actions are better placed to help employees manage mental health, wellbeing, and stress levels. Once 'buried in our work' though, our brains are activated in the prefrontal cortex region again, which depletes the chances of rumination or baseline state of thinking about our social lives, social connections, networks, and activity that can potentially lead to negative consequences.

For leaders wanting to engage and motivate their teams to perform, trust cannot be built when fear is present; therefore, leaders must be able to recognise fear in employees, as well as understanding the potential triggers that may evoke a fear response so they can be addressed. When we are in a state of distrust we experience an 'amygdala hijack' that invokes a rush of cortisol and adrenaline.

Leaders who intentionally create connection and collaboration in teams, by building trust, reducing ambiguity, and using real stories with emotion (rather than corporate speak, facts, figures, and jargon) have the potential to significantly improve relationships, reduce stress, improve learning, and increase followership.

In a state of trust, we feel safe and positive and produce more oxytocin and dopamine—the neurotransmitters that help us relax and feel open to others. We are more capable of innovation, making good decisions and showing more compassion to others. As a result, we partner and connect with others more deeply.

Undertaking the process of recalibration helps leaders to build transparency and respect as well as being able to move closer to creating a vision of shared success.

Know your key stakeholders

As you move through the recalibration process, be clear on who your key stakeholders are. Do you know all of them? Who is going to be pivotal to your success? Know the role of each stakeholder as well. Who are your game changers, decision makers, and influencers? Who do you need for support or to build connection with those you don't know?

Purpose: what are my intentions?

When leaders are looking to recalibrate, the focus starts with why—becoming conscious to what it is that they're doing. What is my purpose? What are my intentions? By tuning in to context in this way, they, all of a sudden, are more mindful and present in the moment. They've tuned in their ability to connect with other human beings. This also helps to mitigate unnecessary drama.

Perception: what is my impact?

Few leaders take the time to reflect on how they are perceived by others in the organisation or externally to their organisation. Understanding the perception that others may hold of them, or of the situation is essential. This is why *listening to connect* is so important. It enables a leader to discover any 'change gaps' that need addressing to ensure our communication and messaging is landing effectively. Understanding these change gaps allows a leader to pivot in the moment so that they're able to have more impact and influence in their leadership.

Perspectives: do you see what I see?

Perspective taking is the ability to comprehend and take on the point of view of another person—how they think and feel and their beliefs around experiences. It can move us closer to others and help us take a *reality check* of situations, people or decisions we need to make. This is where having clarity on your key stakeholders' matters the most.

The ability to consider other perspectives is fundamental to leadership and drawing people closer to strategic solutions. The ability to do a 'reality check' as a habit and to think about the perspective of others is when leaders have a sharpened ability to influence. In The Neuroscience of Strategic Leadership article by Jeffrey Schwartz, Josie Thomson, and Art Kleiner, they talk about mentalising, which is the ability to take on the perspective of others, to think about how they may react to situations. Is there a better way for them to do this? When they're doing this, they're operating from what they call the *high road*. They're using the wise advocate components of the brain that's likely to lead them to leveraging the impacts they want in the future.

I worked with a coachee who went through a similar process when she left her organisation to take up a role. However, within three months, she realised that the promises made by the CEO were not quite available, and this totally changed her feeling about the role. She wasn't able to make the changes that were needed. She tried every element of regulating emotions, of having the conversations and recalibrating her view on ways to approach the situation.

The power of this perspective taking is that it allows someone like this coachee to recognise when a company is not the right one for them. Instead of staying, working in angst and losing self-confidence, she realised she had tried every avenue and that, in reality, the organisation was not going to change. As a result, she was able to move on to her next opportunity. While incredibly disappointed that things didn't work out, she said, at the time, the greatest thing for her was that she knew, in her heart, she was doing the right thing, that she'd given it a go, and she'd learnt a lot from that particular situation. She'd applied a growth mindset, made the changes required, and continued to move forward, and accelerate.

This ability to have power within and a certainty around decision making means that we have less angst and much more conviction in our decision making and ability to move forward. The reality check of this process enables us to consider questions like, who holds the truth? It's time to do a reality check, and this is one of the greatest questions that you can ask in assessing what's really going on, but also in releasing a need to be right, which, as human beings, we can be addicted to.

Purpose-driven leaders ask the hard questions to make decisions more effectively and efficiently. They're clear on the facts. They're clear on what information will enable them to make strategic decisions in the future.

Possibilities: taking strategic action to move forward

This process of recalibrating is the thing that really leads to setting the foundations for strategic action and influence. What is possible with this new insight? Possibility is the framework for those who are stepping up in their leadership, who feel authentic in being who they are because they have a power within and a clarity of mind that allows them to move forward.

The other benefit of recalibrating is the ability to use feed forward. This is allowing people to look at the change gaps, to think about what needs to change moving forward rather than criticising what's happened in the past?

(((↯))) TUNE IN:

To your purpose:

What are your intentions? What outcome are you seeking?

Before meetings, major decisions, or change, make sure you are clear on your intentions. What is your why? If you are caught up 'in the story', then you are less likely to discover truth.

To perceptions:

What impact are you having on others and the situation?

What needs to change?

What needs to stay the same?

What might you need to believe to move forward?

Are you attached or committed?

To perspectives:

What are your insights? What intelligence have you gathered? Is there a better way? What assumptions have you made?

If you had no vested interest in this, how would you look at it?

Learn to 'mentalise' how others may respond. Anticipate what they might need. Keep it safe and keep it simple.

Seek alternatives and tap into the principles of persuasion by Dr Robert Cialdini, an expert in influence.

To what's possible:

What is possible now you have this information and insight? What needs to happen next? What do you want to create? What will activate this possibility?

Use this intelligence to take action. Put together a strategic plan of action to make progress.

Connect with those who matter. Be present.

My self-assessment and actions

_____

_____

_____

_____

_____

_____

_____

_____

_____

_____

_____

_____

_____

_____

_____

NINE

Radiate: Expansive personal leadership

'The need to manage oneself is creating
a revolution in human affairs.'
—Peter Drucker

Abundant
Leading others: leading a group of people or
an organisation with shared vision, an ability
to step up during tough times and an ability
to navigate these times creatively using social
influence. When people follow willingly and
maximise their efforts to achieve the goal.
Conscious competence and unconscious
competence with a willingness to repeat
the cycle of learning as required.

For a long time I have been fascinated with the concept of power and its influence on leadership. In many ways I feel blessed that I have had the opportunity to see how power and leadership can play out in the corporate world, as well as how it plays out in developing countries and governments. Like most of you, I have also experienced the worst of leadership when power is used for personal privilege and people and organisaitons suffer as a result.

Having insight into leadership through the lens of my coaching clients is an incredible privilege that I never take for granted. Each session offers me another lesson on the very real challenges my clients face every single day. The practical way in which to navigate leadership for the 21st century is my obsession. Leaders understand the concepts, but they struggle with the execution.

There is such a cynicism around leadership in Australia right now. Political leaders are thrust into the world of social media and 24-hour news cycles and face new pressures that our leaders in the 80s and 90s couldn't have imagined. This same paradigm is crippling our corporate, community, and sporting leaders.

In a world of 'not enough' and 'us and them', leaders with the ability to navigate a world where everything is speeding up need strategies for slowing things down and being transparent. By this, I don't mean taking longer to respond to people and situations, I mean taking time out to reflect—having the wherewithal to pause and get present in the moment, and to take on the perspective of others and be comfortable questioning your own beliefs, knowing that ultimately you have the power to choose those beliefs at any time.

Expansive leadership is grounded in the ability to be comfortable as a leader in a 'power with others' paradigm. This can only be achieved if the hard inner-work of this book becomes a habit—something that you continually do as a leader.

The Story of Coumba Ndieye, Senegal

Coumba is the epitome of leading through a 'power with others' approach. As a young girl she was only educated to the end of primary school, yet through The Hunger Project training she's transformed her life and is now a senior leader in a national body governing development in Senegal.

Using loans from the rural bank in her early years, she created a small fabric trading business that grew over time. Now she has her own home and her two children study at university. In her government role she has trained more than 5000 women to create and run their own successful businesses. She also trains other leaders within the village and has travelled to other communities to share the learnings.

She has a vision to expand the food processing unit run by a local women's group at Coki, so they can build their export capabilities. Her focus is on partnerships with supermarkets overseas, and when she retires she knows that there are plenty of others capable of taking her place.

The Mayor of Koki described her as *the lion*. When we asked her about leadership and lifting others up, her advice (in Wolof, the local language) was "yawou, yawou, yawou", which translates to *wake up, wake up, wake up* to the possibilities. Lift the most unfortunate and underprivileged along with you.

When walking around the village with Coumba, I realised she is the embodiment of expansive leadership founded on a mindset of abundance and possibility. When women whom she had trained were speaking, Coumba stayed to the side and ensured through body language and adjustment of her clothing that she was out of the limelight.

When the women had finished speaking, and we were being lead to another part of the village she stood tall and resumed her 'lead' role. Her ability to adapt and change how she showed up in different circumstances showed 'power with' leadership. The ripple effect of Coumba's work goes beyond the 5,000 women she has trained—it extends to their families and the people in their communities.

Power **with** others vs power **over** others

'Nearly all men can stand adversity,
but if you want to test a man's
character, give him power.'
—Abraham Lincoln

The ability for a leader to demonstrate 'power with', shows a leader who is abundant in mindset and action. They empower those around them to step up even when they fear failure or loss of control.

Letting go doesn't have to mean 'losing control'. The ability to shift into a conversation that is centred in shared discovery requires a leader to develop 'power with' skills. In a Ted Talk by David Marquet at TEDxScottAFB on how great leaders serve others, he talks about how people gain agency when they are given control or autonomy. In this talk, he discusses the challenges and dangers faced by a submarine crew trained for compliance combined with a leader who is inexperienced on the vessel operating from a traditional command and control style of leadership. By giving agency and reviewing the practices that were implemented, the crew stepped up in its leadership.

Examples like Coumba and David demonstrate the impact of a leader who is conscious and decisive vs reactionary and inconsistent. When the light within us is stronger than the need for light to be upon us, as leaders we achieve the following:

Get out of the way: *Knowing when to let others step into the light*

This is a huge differentiator between a leader who exerts power over vs power with others. Leaders who know when to let others 'step up' into in the light, create a succession plan and path for their people to expand. They give them autonomy and the room to stretch and grow as people.

This opportunity also helps others grow in their own leadership. It gives visibility to those who otherwise often work behind the scenes. If a leader has a fixed mindset, it's likely that they will limit those reporting to them, as they will potentially see them as a threat to their leadership.

Entrusting your people to step into the light, is an opportunity for them to learn, expand, and grow. Give credit to the people in your team for what they are contributing. If you are taking all the credit for those working with you, chances are you are deeply insecure in your leadership, and while you think it may not show, more often than not, you will be found out.

Recognise people for their contributions and openly give credit to all involved so they can advance too.

Gratitude: *Knowing when to shine the light on others*

Gratitude is one of the most powerful actions a leader can take, to remain gracious and humble. Dacher Keltner, professor of psychology at University of California, Berkeley, has studied power in the context of leadership and Lord Acton's belief that 'power does tend to corrupt' (Keltner, 2016). When leaders let power go to their head as they climb the ladder, inevitably "the abuse of power ultimately tarnishes the reputations of those executives, undermining their opportunities for influence".

Practicing gratitude in the 'small moments' is expansive in its impact. I remember one Christmas, I received a hand-written letter of thanks from my CEO. It was unexpected and incredibly appreciated at the time as it had been a tough year in the organisation.

Another example of the power of 'small moments' came when I was in Malawi working with The Hunger Project. Rowlands Kaotcha the Country Director for Malawi met with a colleague and I, late afternoon on a Sunday to plan the week ahead. When we met with Rowlands the next morning to meet his team, he told us about his family and the conversation they had together when he returned home Sunday night. His wife Sphewe was trying to get the kids to bed, but Rowlands decided that even though it was late, as a family they should spend half an hour talking about their day, even if it meant a later bed time for his children who were aged 10 and 12 years at the time.

Rowlands kicked off the conversation and said, "Sphewe, my beautiful wife, tell me about your day". Sphewe replied, "It was fine". The conversation was about to continue but his son interrupted. "Mum, that is not acceptable. You didn't give any detail and Dad built you up, he described you as his beautiful wife and you just *dropped the moment*".

Rowlands and his wife were a little puzzled as they had never heard this expression before. When the children retired to bed, he Googled the expression and couldn't find anything.

I love the conversation shift this created and I've thought about the wisdom of this incredible 10-year-old boy. How often do we all potentially *drop the moment* with our loved ones or our work colleagues because we're too busy or aren't present with each other. When we aren't present we are missing opportunities to elevate and connect with each other. Gratitude is a powerful connector that helps leaders *elevate others in the moment.*

In *The Big Small* (Martin, et al., 2014) the authors talk about the 'small moments' by acknowledging that saying 'thank you' is an opportunity that many miss. As Australians, how often do we say *no worries* when, in fact, a more apt response may be, *I really value our working relationship, so it's my pleasure.* Think about the impact of that small change, delivered in an authentic way with your customers and work colleagues. It might feel strange at first, but the dividends long term are worth it.

Brené Brown also talks about small moments based on her research that shows trust is built on small moments such as stopping to talk to someone when you can see they are upset, even if it means having to put down or stop what you are engrossed in. Or attending the funeral of a team member's family as a show of your support. Think about the areas where you can elevate others in the small moments. Often the small amount of effort it takes to be of service to others, is the difference between average and expansive leadership.

Grace: *Knowing how to shine the light on deflected accountability*

In leadership, there are times when the light must be shone on deflected accountability. This by no means equates to shaming another person. What it does mean, however, is that human beings love comfort zones, and when effort and challenges appear they may seek to deflect responsibility by taking the problem to their leader without a solution. Sometimes this is referred to as 'passing the bomb' and many leaders without adequate training get into the habit of taking the responsibility on themselves. As a result, they begin the cycle of taking on too much, disempowering their people and feeling overwhelmed.

Shining the light on deflected accountability can be done with grace by using reframing coaching techniques. For example, 'I don't have time' may be reframed with the question 'what can you do with the time you have?' or 'what do you need to let go of to give this priority?' Addressing these issues as they arise and asking questions that put accountability firmly back on the other person are ways to ensure that the people you lead lift up. These questions empower people to find solutions, or for those who are deliberately avoiding accountability, they lead to clarity on expectations and minimise the need for performance management situations that often occur when accountability isn't maintained.

Grace also applies to creating an inclusive culture in organisations. Google's *Project Aristotle* study discovered that psychological safety is the number one attribute of a high performing team. This means that people have an equal voice in the organisation and aren't fearful of speaking up. There are times when people express themselves in ways that cause offence to others, sometimes without knowledge of their impact. In Brene Brown's, *Braving the Wilderness* (Brown, 2017) she describes the importance of leaders holding people accountable without shaming them. Grace in leadership is essential to creating this environment of trust and accountability without appearing weak.

Growth: *Knowing how to pivot when your light inside is dimmed*

Leadership is not perfect, and it's delusional not to expect days when you feel like the light within you is dimmed. Sometimes that can happen rapidly, and other times that feeling can creep up on you when you least expect it. Remember that the best leaders see leadership as a continual evolution of learning. The learnings never stop and when your light is dimmed, it may be time to reconnect back to 'triaging your leadership' by reconnecting and checking in on what may be missing.

Have your values changed or shifted in recent months? Have there been life circumstances that have forced you to reassess, realign and take action on a different path again? Is your self-care regime falling to the wayside?

Time for reflection is a habit that all leaders need to practice regularly. Without it, not only will your light dim, but your insights will also. Develop, design, deliver, and dream.

Gravitas: *Knowing when to step into the light*

There are times, as a leader, when you need to step into the light and take control. This is when the presence of a leader is called upon to influence, be the spokesperson for the team or organisation and step up. This is when storytelling is most crucial in communicating your vision and the role your people play in that. Hope and stability are important for people when times are changing rapidly or there is a feeling of uncertainty. Your role, as a leader during these times, requires you to step into the light.

It is also needed when sharing a vision that others may not see yet. Like a lighthouse, it is during the dark that your light is needed most to create a safe harbour. The times when you need to step into the light are:

- During times of uncertainty.
- When communication may have broken down.
- To rally people towards a common goal.
- When it is time to call the 'elephant' in the room.
- To speak up about behaviour that won't be tolerated.

The ability to dial up and dial down power and big egos is essential to using power wisely in your leadership. Leadership requires a strong sense of self, which is above the line in leadership. It drops below the line of behaviour when ones own needs overtake the needs of others. The difference of expansive personal leadership is the ability to recognise when ego kicks in, so you can dial it down when it stops you showing up in service of others.

Congruence: Aligning mind and body

Just like stars aligning, congruence with your mind and body is an important aspect of building trust as a leader of others. Leaders with relationship challenges often have a congruence issue that creates a barrier against their ability to connect with another person. For example, if you are interacting with someone you find challenging and your focus is on that state, then it is likely you will have an interaction that isn't productive or connected. Becoming congruent requires alignment of your five V's:

1. Vitality: how you show up, your energy.
2. Visceral impact: the way others feel when they are around you.

3. Visual impression: the mark you make through visual cues.

4. Verbal impact: what you say and don't say.

5. Value delivered: your service to others.

Vitality

Personal leadership requires the ability to show up, even when you don't feel like it. Managing your energy levels and being conscious of how you show up matters. People notice the energy of leaders and will make assumptions and judgments of you in the small moments. Be conscious of how you show up; your energy can lead to others mirroring you so your vitality should be congruent with your desired reputation as a leader.

Visceral impact

Maya Angelou most famously quoted, 'I've learned that people will forget what you said, people will forget what you did, but people will never forget how you made them feel'. Great intentions are meaningless if your actions speak of the opposite. As a leader, you have a responsibility to create a safe working environment. This creates high performance, so be aware of the way your presence and behaviour makes others feel.

Visual impression

What do people see when you show up? Your visual expression of leadership should meet your aspirations. For example, when I left the corporate sector and started my practice, it was important to be professional but also to demonstrate warmth as a coach and mentor. For example, power suits can potentially isolate people who wish to work with me in a coaching context, so I often deliberately ensure my style is professional and warm because that is the reputation I want to create. However, for others, their aspirations may be all about a power suit. There isn't a right or wrong, but you need to consider whether your visual impression matches your aspirations, and if you aren't congruent, your physiology will be off centre and your impression as a leader may fall short of where you would like it to be.

Your visual impression is also about your body language: what people see you doing in meetings, networking engagements etc. I have seen leaders who roll their eyes in meetings, and I'm sure they are not even aware they are doing it. Become conscious of what your body is doing: this is where being present to your physiology matters so much. As Amy Cuddy discovered in her research, being present is the conduit to trust. This starts with you first. Begin to pay attention to your physical presence. Without even realising it, if your body language is closed, you may be giving off an impression of low power or disinterest.

Verbal impact

What you say and what you 'don't say' can reveal more than you realise. Start to pay attention to your words, tone, and delivery. This also includes being aware of words spoken out of context or overshared, as well as those written in social media platforms. Words matter and as Judith E Glaser would say, 'they create worlds'. Pay attention to how you speak and of what you speak. Learn to suspend judgment and get curious about others. Are the words you speak aligning to your desired positioning as a leader? When you ask questions, are you opening up connection with others or are you engaging in positional conversations that can often unintentionally move to 'tell, sell, yell' syndrome? Refine the art of your conversations and acquire some coaching skills to improve your ability to step up and lead with 'power with' approaches.

Value delivered

While many leaders initially feel they are not delivering the long-term value they crave, especially when working with an organisation for the first time or in a long while, a focus on service assists leaders to be congruent in their intentions and actions as well as ensuring they have their best value offer placed at the table. Your influence as a leader grows when you can demonstrate the value you add in your role or business. More importantly, a 'rising tide lifts all boats'—start to build the capacity in others. Value will continue to be a focus for the future of work, so make sure you let others know about your work and what is in it for them. People who are reliable are valuable.

🔊 TUNE IN:

The 'power with' paradigm: Which of the 'G's do you need to practice or implement more often? Is there anything you need to let go of so you can step up and be expansive in your leadership of others?

Aligning your 5 V's:

Vitality: how you show up matters. Start to pay attention to your energy, and if you feel it dip for more than a few days at a time, then ensure you are taking action to rectify the situation before it becomes a habit.

Visceral impact: start to ask people for forward-focused feedback. How do they feel working with you? How do they feel when they work with you?

Value: learn to speak up about the value you offer in your leadership. You don't have to go it alone, so be sure to stay in touch with those who also want you to do well. Is there an avenue there to grow your value and worth in the market place?

Visual impression: get clear on your aspirations. Your visual impression needs to map your destination.

Verbal impact: mean what you say, and get clear on when you 'are not speaking up'. What may be holding you back from that?

Start to focus on the ripple effect you want to create as a legacy of your leadership. Expansive leadership requires a consistent focus on being congruent as a leader, and showing up with the power within to lead others. Maybe you haven't thought about your legacy as a leader yet.

- 💡 Who will you serve?

- 💡 What is your vision for yourself in the future?

- 💡 How will you show up and step up? The world needs your leadership.

My personal leadership vision

A final note

Personal leadership is the most difficult leadership of all. It takes courage, commitment, and continual evolution and growth. The freedom that comes with unlocking your capacity and leveraging this is worth the effort.

There is a lot of information contained within this book. It may feel overwhelming to many. As you take action, remember the mantra 'progress beats perfection'. You don't have to do this alone. Wake up to the fact that tiny tweaks can result in big changes over time. If you let go of a habit or mindset that isn't working for you, dare to take on a new challenge or decide to take action on one item at a time, then you are on your way to being a better leader of yourself and others.

My hope is that this book has awakened you to what is possible for you. There is a leader within all of us. Let's all choose to find them so we can radiate for others and ourselves.

About the author

Speaker | Author | Mentor | Facilitator | Executive Coach | Trainer

Belinda Brosnan is a leading change agent and thinker on mindset, and personal leadership through change, uncertainty, and complexity. Obsessed with practical solutions for her clients so they can create inclusive and progressive working environments, Belinda is passionate about challenging the patterns of thinking and behaviour that hold people back from being effective collaborators, managers, leaders, and decision makers.

Formerly a senior leader in property development and media industries, Belinda now works extensively with senior leaders and their teams as a mentor, facilitator, trainer, advisor, and speaker. She has completed her NeuroLeadership Certificate with distinction and is an enhanced practitioner in CIQ-Conversational Intelligence.

As a professional certified coach (PCC) with the International Coaching Federation, Belinda has worked with more than 1000 managers and leaders in personal leadership, conversational intelligence and the ability to influence down, across and up in their organisations. She has helped countless leaders discover their true power and their courage to take calculated risks such as changing careers or stepping up to the next level in their current roles.

Belinda is also an advocate and investor with The Hunger Project and has led leadership immersion programs in Uganda, Malawi, India, and Senegal. She is passionate about being a voice for those who don't have one and giving people the opportunity to lead an expansive life on their terms for the betterment of others, organisations, and communities.

Belinda was the QLD Telstra Business Women's Awards winner for Start-Up in 2015.

Work with me

EXECUTIVE COACHING & MENTORING

Belinda works with a limited number of executives to help them expand their thinking, bring their best selves to their leadership and show up authentically through change, uncertainty, and complexity.

LEADERSHIP DEVELOPMENT PROGRAMS

Belinda works closely with leadership teams to cut through the fluff and deliver programs with real results. Leadership for the 21st century needs tuned-in leaders who are willing to step up, lead and drive high performing teams and inclusive cultures and to think expansively in changing times.

For more information about Belinda's programs for individuals, teams and organisations go to www.belindabrosnan.com or email belinda@belindabrosnan.com or phone +61437728792

Belinda is a person of great energy, high integrity and has a focus on getting results. I have seen her do this through a strengths-based collaborative approach that recognises that organisational culture is the key and we need to do things differently... She is a forthright, strategic thinker, who walks the talk.
Narelle Hooper, Author & Editor in Chief, Company Director

Connect with me on LinkedIN for further testimonials: www.linkedin.com/in/belindabrosnan

References

Brown, B., 2015. *Daring greatly: How the courage to be vulnerable transforms the way we live, love, parent, and lead.* s.l.:Avery.

Brown, B., 2017. *Braving the wilderness: The quest for true belonging and the courage to stand alone.* s.l.:Random House.

Bryant, A. & Kazan, A. L., 2012. *Self-leadership: How to become a more successful, efficient and effective leader from the inside out.* s.l.:McGraw-Hill Education.

Coleman, D., 2005. *Emotional Intelligence: Why it can matter more than IQ.* 10th Anniversary ed. s.l.:Bantam Books.

Collins, J. & Hansen, M. T., 2011. *Great by choice.* s.l.:HarperBusiness.

Cuddy, A., 2015. *Presence: Bringing your boldest self to your biggest challenges.* s.l.:Little, Brown and Company.

Drew, T. & Wolfe, J., 2013. The invisible gorilla strikes again: Sustained inattentional blindness in expert observers.

Dweck, C. S., 2006. *Mindset: The New Psychology of Success.* NY: Random House Publishing Group.

Gallup, 2013. *State of the global workplace,* s.l.: s.n.

Garner, J., 2017. *It's who you know: How a network of 12 key people can fast-track your success.* QLD: John Wiley & Sons Australia Ltd.

George, B., 2015. *Discover your true north: Becoming an authentic leader.* s.l.:Jossey-Bass.

Huffington, A., 2015. *Thrive: The third metric to redefining success and creating a life of well-being, wisdom, and wonder.* s.l.:Harmony.

Jacobs, T., 2016. *Pacific Standard.* [Online]
Available at: https://psmag.com/social-justice/creativitys-underappreciated-component-persistence

Keltner, D., 2016. Don't let power corrupt you. *Harvard Business Review*, October.

Martin, S. J., Goldstein, N. & Cialdini, R., 2014. *The small big: Small changes that spark big influence.* s.l.:Grand Central Publishing.

McEvoy, S., Stevenson , M. & Woodward, M., 2007. *The contribution of passengers versus mobile phone use to motor vehicle crashes resulting in hospital attendance by hte driver,* s.l.: Accidents, analysis and prevention.

Pink, D., 2011. *Drive: The surprising truth about what motivates us.* s.l.:Riverhead Books.

Rath, T., 2009. *Strengths based leadership: Great leaders, teams and why people follow.* 1st ed. s.l.:Gallup Press.

Schwartz, J. M., 2012. *You are not your brain: The 4-step solution for changing bad habits, ending unhealthy thinking, and taking control of your life.* s.l.:Avery.

Schwartz, J., Thomson, J. & Kleiner, A., 2016. The neuroscience of strategic leadership. *strategy+business*, 5 December.

www.ingramcontent.com/pod-product-compliance
Lightning Source LLC
Chambersburg PA
CBHW071557200326
41519CB00021BB/6796